More
Science Experiments
You Can Eat

More
Science Experiments
You Can Eat

by Vicki Cobb

illustrated by Giulio Maestro

J. B. Lippincott   New York

The author extends grateful appreciation to a friend at General Foods and to Earl J. Merwin at McCormick & Co., Inc.

Copyright © 1979 by Vicki Cobb
Illustrations copyright © 1979 by Giulio Maestro
All Rights Reserved
Printed in the United States of America
6 8 9 7 5

U.S. Library of Congress Cataloging in Publication Data

Cobb, Vicki.
 More science experiments you can eat.

 SUMMARY: Experiments with food demonstrate various scientific principles and produce eatable results. Includes beef jerky, cottage cheese, synthetic cola, and pudding.
 1. Science—Experiments—Juvenile literature. 2. Cookery—Juvenile literature. [1. Science—Experiments. 2. Cookery] I. Maestro, Giulio. II. Title.
 Q164.C5   502'.8   78–12732
 ISBN-0-397-31826-6   ISBN-0-397-31853-7 (pbk)
 ISBN-0-397-31878-2 (LB)

For Ed, finally

Contents

More
Science Experiments
You Can Eat

1

Meanwhile, Back at the Lab . . .

Your kitchen laboratory holds unlimited possibilities for adventure! The cupboard is far from bare when it comes to investigating nature with food. So it's time to return to every home's built-in laboratory, the place that has the materials, equipment, water, heat source, and refrigeration found in any professional laboratory worth its salt.

If you have reservations about your ability as a scientist, relax. Science is not the mysterious process for eggheads it's cracked up to be. And that's what this book will show you. It will introduce you to a new way of looking at something familiar. (In a well-fed nation like ours, it's hard to find many things much more familiar than food.) There is excitement in looking at familiar stuff in a new way, a way that tells you something about the nature of the material, how it came to be, how it changes, and how we sense these changes. Underneath all the apparent confusion of change are basic and unchanging laws of nature. Discovering the unchanging through the study of change is what makes science creative and sometimes thrilling.

FOOD AS A SUBJECT FOR SCIENCE

No living organism can survive very long without food. It serves two main functions: it provides the raw materials for growth and replacement of living substances, and the energy necessary for all life functions. Living organisms are highly organized, always changing, delicately balanced chemical systems. This means that living materials are made up of the same basic stuff or *elements* as nonliving materials. The smallest particles of these elements, *atoms*, are arranged in combinations making larger particles called *molecules*. Most of the molecules of living things—carbohydrates, fats, and proteins—are quite complicated, much more complicated than the molecules of the nonliving world. And the organization of these molecules into even the simplest living cell is so intricate that it is still not completely understood. But we do understand that, if an organism is to survive, this high-level organization must be constantly maintained against the natural forces that tend toward disorganization. Food, among other things, is required if life is to continue.

All living things are roughly divided into two groups, according to how they get food. The *autotrophs* (from Greek words meaning "self-nourishing") make their own nutrients as part of their life process. Autotrophs include all green plants and green microorganisms (one-celled plants); they manufacture sugar (a basic foodstuff) from the simpler molecules of carbon dioxide and water. Many plants then build sugar molecules into larger and more complicated starch molecules. Autotrophs are the bottom link of what is called the food chain; all other living things depend on autotrophs, either directly or indirectly, as a food source.

All other living things are *heterotrophs* ("other-nourishing"), organisms that do not generate their own food but consume autotrophs or other heterotrophs. This group is made up of all animals, including humans; most microorganisms; and all nongreen plants. The bodies of all heterotrophs produce special substances called *enzymes* for digestion of food. Digestion is the process of breaking down the complex molecules in food into simpler molecules that can then be used as a source of energy to keep the life processes going, or as the basic materials for building our own particular varieties of proteins, fats, and carbohydrates.

But digestion is not part of the subject matter of this book. There are many changes in food long before our digestive juices get a chance to work on it. Food preparation creates changes in food. And if certain foods are simply allowed to stand around, changes occur. In general, foods are rapidly changing chemical systems that interact with air, water, other foods, chemicals, and microorganisms. The interactions are affected by conditions of heat and atmospheric moisture. Rapidly changing chemical systems are obviously a scientist's "meat" that can satisfy some of our hunger for knowledge. In *Science Experiments You Can Eat,* the focus was on using food to understand basic scientific principles. In this book the emphasis is shifted. You will be using principles of science to investigate food.

The Proof of the Pudding . . .

Experiments are the basis of scientific investigation. They are tests for determining if one particular factor causes a particular change. You can, for example, do a simple experiment to see if baking powder is an essential part of a cake. Prepare two identical batters, but leave the baking powder out of one of them. Bake the batters in the same kind of pan at the same temperature for the same period of time. In other words, everything about the two potential cakes is exactly the same except for the presence of baking powder. Then, if there is a difference in the outcome, you can safely assume that the cause of this difference was the baking powder factor. In this case, the difference will be readily observable. One cake will be light and spongy. The other will be firm, flat, and very uncakelike. Both will be completely edible, as the title of this book suggests. Whether you choose to eat them or not is up to you. Be warned at the outset: This book is *not* a cookbook, and the results of these experiments will not constitute gourmet dining. But all of them will provide some nourishment and can be eaten without worry (except where specific warnings to the contrary are given).

Differences in the results of experimental procedures in science are detected by a process called *measurement*. The word "measurement" probably discourages many potential scientists. It suggests mathematics, which many people find frightening. It's true that if you wish to become a nuclear physicist you must know some sophisticated mathematics. However, there is a great deal of measurement in science that does not involve any math whatsoever. Believe it or not, detecting the difference between our two cakes is a kind of measurement—the simplest kind, as you will see. Perhaps if science with this kind of measurement captures your imagination, you won't find it threatening to learn the math needed for more complicated science.

In any event, we'll be dealing with three kinds of measurement here:

Measurement on the *nominal* (or naming) scale is simply identifying whether or not a phenomenon exists. The results of the experiment with the cakes are measured on the nominal scale. Baking powder is identified (named) as the factor affecting the texture of the cakes.

Things measured on the *ordinal* scale are ranked as greater or lesser than one another. But there is no way of telling *how much* greater or lesser. You can rank bananas on an ordinal scale according to ripeness by comparing how green, yellow, or brown they are. But you cannot say a brown banana is twice as ripe as a yellow one.

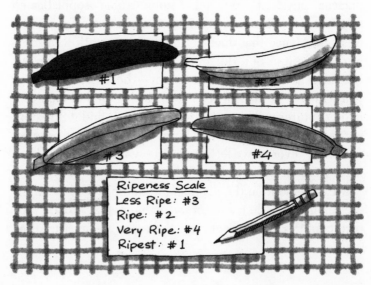

The *interval* scale puts numbers on the ranking. Most of what you might consider everyday types of measurement—temperature, length, and weight—are on interval scales. Interval scales tell *how much* because the intervals (or spaces) between numbers are equal. That is, the distance between 3 and 4 is the same as the distance between 7 and 8, or 55 and 56.

The more sophisticated a science gets, the more subtle the differences it measures, and the more mathematics is needed to do the measuring. But in this book, we're emphasizing results that are on nominal and ordinal scales. (Occasionally, we get a little more precise and hit the interval scale.) In fact, many experiments are simple comparisons where you determine differences with your senses of sight or taste or smell. And often the proof will be in the eating.

How to Do an Experiment

To get the most out of this book, you should know *what* you are doing in each experiment and *why* you are doing it. Every chapter has a short introduction that discusses the subject you will be investigating. Every experiment also has a short introduction that asks a question you can answer by doing the experiment. Most of the experiments are open-ended; that is, they are the beginning of what may turn out to be a fascinating and continuing series of studies. The idea is to launch you on investigative adventures rather than only to give quick answers to experimental questions.

The materials and equipment needed for each experiment are listed at the beginning. Read through the entire experiment and collect everything you need before you begin a procedure. This way you will not be caught without something important at a critical time during the experiment.

The procedure section tells you how to do the experiment. Often the reasons for doing a certain step are discussed as you go along. Since timing is important, again, you should read through the procedure before you attempt it. Procedures are the heart of a scientific experiment. Good procedures give clear-cut results that answer the question raised at the outset.

The procedures in this book have all been tested. But they are by no means the last word. If you can think of a better way to answer an experimental question, if you wish to change a procedure, go to it! If there are any rules here, the main one is that *there are no hard and fast rules*. Science would not grow if people followed procedures as if they were unchangeable rituals. In fact, coming up with original procedures is the essence of the creative process in science. The procedures in this book have been designed with this thought in mind.

After the procedure section there is a brief discussion of what to look for in your results and what the results mean. There are also suggestions for follow-up studies.

There are certain standard precautions for safety and for using equipment in every laboratory, and your kitchen is not an exception. Consult the cook in your house before you start experimenting in your kitchen, and ask about any procedures or terms you are not certain about.

2

The Ripening Process

Some foods, such as fruit and cheese, are living systems that change or ripen with time. The ripening process is accompanied by changes in color, texture, odor, and, of course, taste. Ripening changes increase the desirability of these foods, but only up to a point. If food is allowed to continue to ripen, spoilage (which is discussed in greater detail in the next chapter) is the ultimate result.

Whenever easily observable changes occur, you can be sure you have good subject matter for scientific investigation. Ripening is affected by a number of factors. The idea of this chapter is to discover some of these factors in a systematic way.

RIPENING FRUIT

As bananas ripen, the green pigment in the skin, called *chlorophyll*, is broken down chemically and disappears.

19

The yellow pigments, called *carotenes* and *flavones*, which have been there all the time, are revealed with the disappearance of chlorophyll. Chemical changes occur in the flesh of the fruit as well: starch changes to sugar; *pectin* (a carbohydrate found in unripe fruit) breaks down, losing its stiffness; and the flesh softens.

Is ripening fruit a self-contained system, or is the rate of these changes affected by the environment? We designed the following experiment to see if different atmospheres, produced by different packaging, affected the rate of ripening. You will vary the atmosphere surrounding unripe bananas and observe the effect on the ripening process.

Materials and Equipment

> 7 very green bananas
> 1 very ripe banana
> 2 small brown paper bags (lunch-size bags work best)
> a plastic bag and twist fastener
> plastic wrap

Procedure

Set up the bananas in their environments as follows:

1. Put two green bananas in a paper bag and fold the top over several times to seal out the air.
2. Put one green banana and the very ripe banana in the other paper bag and fold over the top.
3. Put two green bananas in a plastic bag. Twist the top and fasten with a twist fastener.

4. Wrap one green banana in several layers of plastic wrap. Make sure it is sealed tightly at each end.
5. Leave one green banana exposed to the air.

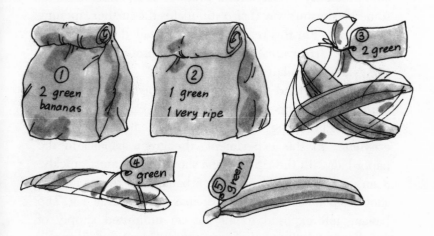

Leave the fruit alone for four or five days to ripen. Do not open any of the bags during this period. Then examine all the fruit. Which fruit is still green? Which is most yellow? Which has the most brown? You can eat the ripe bananas or put them back and allow the experiment to continue for another day or so.

Observations

Which banana ripened most quickly? Which banana turned brown fastest? Did the ripe banana have an effect on the rate at which the unripe banana ripened? What evidence is there that ripening fruit somehow changes the environment?

Ripening fruit "breathes" or respires. This means that it takes up oxygen and gives off carbon dioxide. Oxygen is essential for the chemical reactions involved in ripening. In addition, ripening fruit gives off another gas, called *ethylene*. Not only is ethylene a product of ripening fruit; in some mysterious way it also stimulates the further ripening of the fruit. For this reason it has been called the "ripening hormone." (*Hormones* are chemicals produced by living things that stimulate cellular changes.)

Paper bags tend to keep the ethylene in, but they are porous enough to allow oxygen (and ethylene) to pass through. Plastic bags do not allow the free flow of oxygen or ethylene. In this experiment, the green banana in the paper bag with the ripe banana should ripen most quickly. (Can you state why?) The green bananas in the paper bag should ripen faster than the bananas in the plastic bag. The banana left exposed to air has an unlimited supply of oxygen, so it will turn brown most quickly. You will notice that the side of this banana that rests on the counter will ripen more quickly than the other sides, because it has the most intimate contact with its own ethylene. The banana that is tightly wrapped in plastic has no oxygen supply and should ripen most slowly. (However, if all the air is not sealed out of the package, this banana will ripen first—can you see why?) Now can you see why bananas are sealed in plastic in many supermarkets?

For Further Study

The green mold that grows on citrus fruits (for instance, lemons and oranges) gives off so much ethylene that a single moldy lemon has been known to greatly speed up the ripening of five hundred green lemons. If you should come across a moldy lemon, you might want to test its effect on unripe fruit. Put it in a paper bag along with an unripe pear, plum, peach, or avocado.

You have probably heard the old cliché, "A rotten apple spoils the whole barrel." Do your results show how this saying originated?

CULTURED CREAM

Bacteria are living one-celled organisms that need food to grow and multiply. One variety of bacteria, called *lactobacilli*, feeds on milk and is the foundation of the dairy industry.

These rod-shaped microscopic organisms are ordinarily found floating in the air in an inactive, or "latent," state. When they land in some milk, they spring to life, using the sugar in milk as food. Bacteria don't get "fatter" as they take in food; instead, each organism divides in half, and

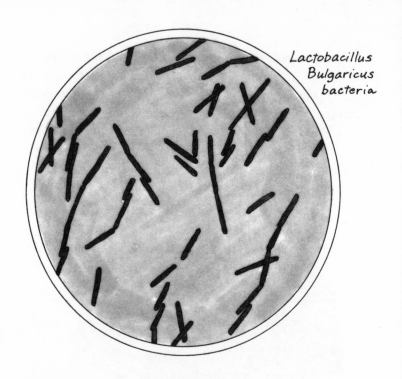

Lactobacillus
Bulgaricus
bacteria

their numbers increase. In the process of growing (that is, multiplying), the lactobacilli give off a waste product called *lactic acid*. This acid has a peculiar effect on milk. Not only does it make milk taste sour (as any acid would), but it causes the protein in milk to coagulate, or become a semisolid mass. Yogurt, sour cream, and many cheeses, called "cultured milk products" (milk products in which bacteria are growing), are the end result of the work of living lactobacilli. These products contain lactobacilli cultures that can be used to "culture" other milk or cream. In this experiment you study the effects of two different starter cultures on heavy cream. The end result is a thick, rich, slightly sour cream that is quite delicious. The French call it *crème fraîche*.

Materials and Equipment

1 pint heavy cream
measuring cup
2 spotlessly clean 1- to 2-cup jars with lids (peanut
    butter jars are good)
cultured buttermilk
sour cream
spoons for stirring
measuring spoons

Procedure

Put 1 cup (½ pint) heavy cream in each jar. Add 1 teaspoon cultured buttermilk to one jar and stir with a clean spoon. Add 1 teaspoon sour cream to the other jar and stir. (The sour cream will be lumpy and will need to be broken up so it will blend in smoothly.) Use a different spoon for each stirring operation. Taste the contents of each jar, using the spoon you stirred it with. *Don't contaminate the jars by putting in a spoon that has been in your mouth. Keep everything as clean as possible.* Don't let anything you have touched with your hands or mouth come in contact with the contents of the jars. Undesirable microbes can grow just as easily as lactobacilli.

Screw the covers of the jars on tightly. Allow them to stand in a warm place overnight. (The top of a dishwasher or other warm appliance works well.) The cream should become too thick to pour; this may take from 16 to 36 hours. The thickness of the cream is considered the "measure of ripeness" of crème fraîche.

Observations

Which crème fraîche is smoother? Which is more sour? Different cultures give the cream different flavors. You will probably prefer one over the other. We liked the buttermilk culture better.

Refrigerate and use within a week. Crème fraîche is especially delicious with fresh fruit and a little sugar. Try some on sliced ripe bananas from the last experiment and add a little brown sugar and cinnamon. Or try some on granola or another cereal.

For Further Study

Try making crème fraîche with a yogurt culture: stir 1 teaspoon of plain yogurt into the heavy cream. Also, try to get similar results from a yeast culture. Mix ¼ teaspoon active dry yeast with 1 tablespoon of warm milk. Add to a cup of heavy cream. Stir, put a lid on the jar, and let stand in a warm place until the cream thickens. How do the yogurt and yeast cultures taste?

Repeat the procedure to see the effect of temperature on bacterial activity. Use a single starter culture, such as yogurt or buttermilk. Set up three samples. Put one jar in the refrigerator; heat one sample to boiling in a saucepan, then pour into a jar and leave at room temperature; keep the third at room temperature overnight. Can you now explain why cultured milk products are sold in a refrigerated state? What effect does boiling have on lactobacilli? You can check this out further by boiling your starter culture and then adding it to new cream. Will it become crème fraîche?

COTTAGE CHEESE: WHOLE VERSUS SKIM MILK

The basis of all cheese is milk solids, the proteins and fats in milk. Milk solids can be separated from the watery portion of milk in several ways. You can add an acid such as lemon juice or vinegar. You can add an enzyme (a protein that controls chemical reactions in living systems) such as *rennet*, the milk-coagulating protein derived from the stomachs of calves. It's used to make Junket desserts. And, of course, you can use a lactobacilli culture. When milk is made into cheese, the milk protein is coagulated and then separated as "curds" from the watery portion of the milk, or "whey." Cottage cheese is one of the simplest fresh cheeses to prepare.

Cottage cheese is almost synonymous with the word "diet." It's a staple food for many people when they want to lose weight. That's because most commercial cottage cheese is made from skim milk, milk with the butterfat removed. In this experiment you make cottage cheese from skim milk and compare it with cottage cheese you make from whole milk. The question you'll be trying to answer is: Does butterfat make a difference in the texture and taste of cottage cheese curds?

The procedures for this experiment and for the next one (making soft- or hard-ripened cheese) lend themselves to an almost unlimited series of other experiments in cheese making. (There are specialists called dairy microbiologists who study the making of cheese and other cultured milk products as a career.) The cottage cheese results of this experiment can serve as the raw material for the one that follows. If you intend to go on and make pressed and ripened cheese, read the instructions for *Hard-Ripened Cheese* and collect all your equipment for both experiments before you start making cottage cheese.

Note: In any cheese-making experiment, there is a possibility that your mixture, instead of ripening, will spoil. This can happen if your equipment isn't perfectly clean, or if the temperature is too high. If your cheese smells bad or looks spoiled, *do not eat it*.

Materials and Equipment

½ gallon skim milk
½ gallon whole milk
2 large glass or ceramic bowls or stainless steel pots
    (don't use aluminum or cast iron)
cultured buttermilk
measuring spoons
plastic wrap
knife
a very large pot and a smaller one (stainless steel) that
    fits inside it—to be used as a double boiler
spoons for stirring
2 small glasses
colander
cheesecloth
2 small bowls
heavy cream or crème fraîche (optional)

Procedure

Allow the cartons of milk to stand, unrefrigerated, for several hours until the milk is at room temperature. Pour the skim milk into one large bowl and the whole milk into the other. Add 3 tablespoons of buttermilk to each and stir well. Cover each bowl with plastic wrap and put the bowls in a warm place overnight.

The next day the milk will be "clabbered," or like a soft custard. (Using what you learned in the *Cultured Cream* experiment, can you explain what causes the milk to clabber?) The milk is ready for the next step if the whey is starting to collect around the edges. If this isn't happening, it isn't "ripe" yet. Give it more time.

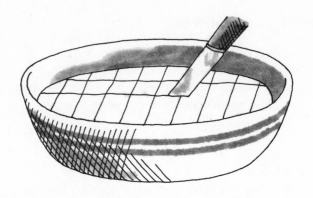

Make slices through the curds one inch apart. Repeat in the other direction to make a crisscross pattern, forming rough cubes.

The next step is to further coagulate the curds and cause them to separate from the whey. This is done by very slow heating to about 100°F (just warm to the touch). If you heat the curds too quickly or to too high a temperature, they will become tough. Put a bowl containing clabbered milk in a pot containing hot water. (If the bowl doesn't fit into the pot, or if it isn't heat-proof, gently pour the curds and whey into a stainless steel saucepan that does fit in the larger pot.) Heat over a very low flame, stirring occasionally. The heating process should take about 30 minutes. Heat until the milk is just warm to the touch.

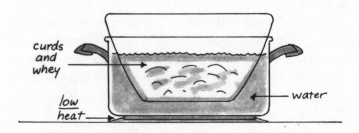

curds and whey

low heat

water

Remove the curds and whey from the heat and let them cool for about 20 minutes. Meanwhile, repeat the procedure with the second batch of clabbered milk.

Skim off about ¼ cup of whey from the first batch of cheese into a small glass. Set aside. Line a colander with two layers of cheesecloth. Pour the curds and whey into the cheesecloth and let drain. From time to time, lift up the cheesecloth and shake the curds to let pockets of trapped whey drain through. Bring the tops of the cheesecloth

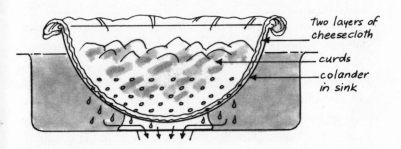

Two layers of cheesecloth

curds

colander in sink

together, twist, and squeeze out the remaining whey. Put the drained curds into a small bowl. (If you wish, you can rinse the curds under cool water. We didn't find this necessary.) Repeat the procedure as precisely as possible for the other batch of cheese.

Observations

Taste the whey samples from both batches. Are they different in appearance and taste? Taste the curds from both batches. Which are more tender? (One standard for judging the quality of cottage cheese is the tenderness of the curd.) Do you think butterfat plays a role in making a more tender curd?

Save the curds from the whole milk for the next experiment, if you wish. If not, salt the curds and mix in heavy cream to taste (or crème fraîche from the last experiment). Refrigerate the cheese until you are ready to eat it. Cottage cheese is perishable and should be eaten within two or three days.

For Further Study

Design an experiment to observe what happens when clabbered curds are heated above 100°F.

Make cottage cheese from straight cultured buttermilk. You can also try different starter cultures, including yogurt and commercial cottage cheese. Clabber milk with acid such as lemon juice or vinegar. Meat tenderizer (actually an enzyme called *papain*) also clabbers milk. Try making cheese with this enzyme.

Rennet tablets are used to make commercial cottage cheese. They are, however, almost impossible to find in supermarkets or drugstores. If you do come across them, it might be fun to try using them for the initial clabbering process.

HARD-RIPENED CHEESE

Cottage cheese is often a stage on the way from milk to what we think of as real cheese—cured and ripened cheese. The ripening process takes anywhere from a few weeks to several years. Some cured and ripened cheeses

are hard, like cheddar cheese; others are semisoft like Brie or Camembert. The taste and texture of a cheese is determined by a number of factors, including the amounts of butterfat and water in the unripe cheese, whether or not the cheese is cooked, and the type of organism doing the ripening.

One of the simplest hard-ripened cheeses to make is Colby cheese. In this experiment, you make a variety of Colby. The main idea is to learn a technique for making hard cheese that can serve as the basis for any number of experiments.

Materials and Equipment

1-pound coffee can and metal top (save the top when you open the can, or use the new top from a freshly opened can)

hammer

large nail

whole milk cottage cheese from the last experiment

cheesecloth

scissors

#2 can, unopened (we used a 20-ounce can of minestrone soup)

weights (we used six very fat cookbooks) or a large C clamp or a handscrew

knife

paper towels

rack

paraffin (optional)

disposable aluminum pie pan (optional)

Procedure

The coffee can is going to be your cheese press. First make drain holes in the bottom. Use the hammer and nail to punch about ten holes in the bottom of the can.

Place freshly made whole milk cottage cheese from the last experiment in cheesecloth and squeeze out as much

whey as possible. Line the coffee can with a double layer of fresh cheesecloth. Put the curds into the can and fold the cheesecloth over the top neatly. (You may have to trim away some of the excess cheesecloth.) Slide the top of the can down on top of the cheese. Put the unopened #2 can on the lid of the coffee can. In a real cheese press, the part that serves the same function as the coffee can top is called the "follower."

Now weight the follower. Pile books on top of the #2 can, or use two flat pieces of wood and a C clamp or handscrew. Place the entire apparatus in the sink or the bathtub, as whey will continue to drain out through the holes.

After a few hours, take the weights off and empty out the whey that has collected in the can on top of the cheese. Reassemble. Keep the cheese weighted overnight.

The next day, remove the cheese. Unwrap it and wash the surface. Cut the cheese in quarters. Wipe each piece dry with paper towels.

Let the cheeses dry on a rack at room temperature for several days. Turn and wipe every day. When the surface has dried out enough, a rind will start to form.

If you wish, you can put a wax rind on the cheese. At the supermarket, buy the paraffin wax used for sealing jelly jars. Ask an adult to help you with the melting; it can be dangerous, since paraffin is highly flammable. Place a block of paraffin in a disposable aluminum pie pan. Set the aluminum pan in a skillet or other pan of water. Heat slowly over a low flame until the paraffin is melted. *Do not place the paraffin pan directly over the flame.* Dip each piece of cheese in the melted paraffin. Remove, let cool, and dip the other side. It may take several dippings to coat the pieces completely.

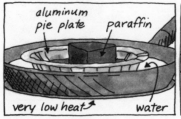

aluminum pie plate — paraffin
very low heat — water

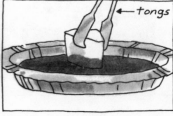

←—tongs

Let the cheeses ripen at room temperature in a dry place. It takes about 30 days for Colby cheeses to fully ripen. After the cheeses have ripened for 10 days, sample one of them. Write down your impressions, using words like "chalky," "bland," "sharp," "hard," "crumbly," etc. Each week, eat one of the other pieces and record your impressions of the taste and texture to see what changes occur over time. The lactobacilli continue to grow during the ripening process, forming waste products that make the cheese delicious.

For Further Study

Use this procedure to make cheese beginning with other starter cultures. Compare cheese made from curds started with yogurt to that made from curds started with buttermilk.

Change the butterfat content of the cheese and see how it affects the final flavor. Make cheese from heavy cream, whole milk, and skim milk. Divide each cheese into quarters before coating with paraffin. Taste samples over a period of time.

You might try rinsing the curds of commercial cottage cheese and using them as your starting point. The butterfat content is very low (4 percent). How does this affect the taste and texture of the finished product?

MOLD-RIPENED CHEESE

Certain molds have been of the utmost importance in making some cheeses world famous. Roquefort, Camembert, and Brie cheeses are all mold-ripened. The molds involved are different species of a blue mold called *Penicillium*. (Yes, it's in the same genus as the mold from which we got the miracle drug penicillin.)

Molds, like mushrooms, are fungi. Both are plant types that do not contain the green pigment chlorophyll. Chlorophyll enables green plants to make their own food (sugars and starches) from carbon dioxide and water. Molds and other fungi cannot do this and must get their food from other substances. That's why they grow on food sources such as trees or bread.

Molds are made up of many cells, unlike bacteria and yeasts, which are single-celled organisms. Mold cells form threadlike structures called *hyphae* (pronounced HIGH-fee) that branch and rejoin to make a tangled mass. It is these threads connecting one microscopic plant to another that distinguish molds from other fungi. Most molds have two kinds of hyphae. *Vegetative hyphae* grow into the host material or lie on its surface. Their job is to get water and nutrients for the plant. *Fertile hyphae* extend into the air and carry the reproductive structures, tiny seedlike items called *spores*. Fertile hyphae give bread mold its fuzzy appearance.

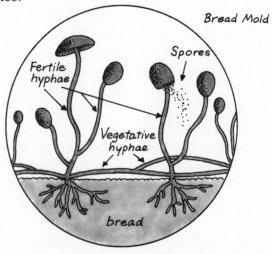

Bread Mold

Spores

Fertile hyphae

Vegetative hyphae

bread

Mold spores are always floating in the air. Although molds are often the cause of food spoilage, they are harmless and can be eaten without danger. In fact, *Penicillium roqueforti* and *Penicillium camemberti* are considered delicious when eaten in cheese. But when they grow on bread (they are the blue bread mold, not the

Penicillium roqueforti

cottony variety), they are considered very unappetizing. The main danger from eating moldy food is that other, harmful microorganisms may have entered the food along with the mold.

In this experiment you will try three different methods of transferring mold cultures from one kind of cheese to another. The challenge is to see if you can get the molds to grow, flourish, and ripen on cheeses normally not the hosts for these molds. In the process you'll discover how molds ripen cheeses. Again, use your judgment about whether ripening or spoilage is taking place. When in doubt, throw it out.

Materials and Equipment

¼ pound Muenster cheese
knife
¼ pound Brie or Camembert
straight pin
waxed paper
measuring spoons
shallow dish
3-ounce package cream cheese
¼ pound Roquefort or blue cheese
tapestry needle (a sewing needle with a very large
    eye)
pencil with an eraser
magnifying glass

Procedure

Cut three cubes of Muenster cheese that are about 1½ inches on each side. The first method of transferring mold culture is the simplest. With a knife, scrape a sliver of mold off the outer surface of the Brie or Camembert. Slide the

mold off the knife onto a Muenster cube. With a pin, punch a lot of air holes in a piece of waxed paper. Wrap the cheese in it for some protection against airborne organisms.

In cheese-manufacturing plants, unripened curd that will become Brie is spread with a thick mixture of water and mold called a slurry. Next, you will try to transfer mold this way. Make a slurry by mixing about ½ teaspoon of mold scrapings with about the same amount of water. In a shallow dish, spread slurry over a cube of Muenster and a piece of cream cheese. Let the water evaporate before wrapping each cube in pinholed wax paper. Keep at room temperature.

The third method of transferring mold culture is by inoculation. You will inoculate a Muenster cube and some cream cheese with the blue *Penicillium* mold from Roquefort or blue cheese. Make an inoculation needle by sticking the point of a tapestry needle into the eraser of a pencil.

Sterilize the end of your inoculation needle (the eye end) by heating it over the burner of your stove until it's red-hot. (This step isn't strictly necessary, as our technique in this experiment is far from being sterile. But it doesn't hurt to learn some professional techniques. Microbiologists use heat to sterilize their wire "loops" or inoculation needles.) Make sure the needle is completely cooled before using it. A red-hot needle will burn the cheese and kill the molds. But don't touch the needle to check its temperature! You could burn yourself, and you could also transfer some germs from your hands to the needle. You can cool the needle quickly without contaminating it by dipping it in water that has been boiled and then cooled.

Punch some holes in the Muenster cube and in the cream cheese with the eye end of the needle. Sterilize the needle again to burn out the cheese caught in the eye. Now scrape up some blue cheese mold with the eye and insert it into a hole. Repeat until you have transferred mold into all the holes. Put some mold on the surface also. Wrap the inoculated cheese in pinholed waxed paper. Keep at room temperature.

Observations

Observe the growth of the molds over the next week or so. Use a magnifying glass. Look for softening of the cheese under the molds and for the appearance of fuzzy fertile hyphae. Smell the ripening cheese. As the mold breaks down the protein in the cheese, amino acids and ammonia form. Ripe mold-ripened cheese has a distinctive ammonia smell.

In the ripening process, molds actually digest the *casein* (milk proteins) in the curd. This changes the consistency of the curd from firm to soft, and eventually to runny. Cheese experts consider a Brie or Camembert cheese to be ripe when the entire cheese has a creamy consistency and no chalky curd is found if the cheese is cut.

For Further Study

Next time you see a commercial Camembert or Brie, look closely at the paper in which it has been wrapped. You will see that it has air holes. As an experiment, wrap inoculated cheese cubes in plastic wrap without air holes. Observe the cheese over the next week or so through the plastic. Don't unwrap and let air in. What effects does oxygen supply have on the ripening process? The molds that produce Roquefort cheese may not need as much oxygen as those that produce Camembert and Brie. Can you design an experiment to test this?

Molds grow best in moderately warm temperatures. Put some inoculated samples in the refrigerator and keep a duplicate set of samples at room temperature. Compare the rate of mold growth. Do you see why grocery stores keep cheeses under refrigeration?

Salt may also affect the growth of some molds. Prepare sets of inoculated cheeses using Roquefort, Camembert, and Brie molds. Salt one set and leave another set unsalted. Which molds are most affected by salt?

You can test the effect of other factors on the growth of mold. To be scientific, be sure to change only one variable at a time. Use the same mold for inoculating, the same cheeses as host materials, and the same procedures for transferring molds.

A French cheese manufacturer moved his factory. The cheese did not ripen properly in the new ripening room. Someone took some cheese made at the old place and rubbed it on the walls in the new room. The problem was solved. Can you think why?

3

Food Preservation

If the ripening process is allowed to continue, or if food is simply left standing around at room temperature for days, weeks, or months, changes continue to occur—and the results are not pleasant. The process you would observe is called *spoilage*. The color, odor, and texture of spoiled food are decidedly unappetizing. In fact, our distaste for spoiled food is nature's way of protecting us from eating it and getting sick. However, the study of spoilage whets the appetite of many serious scientists. The more we understand about how food decays, the better we will be able to deal with decay products in combating pollution and recycling garbage. In this book, though, we promised you edible results, so the theme of this chapter is how to prevent food from spoiling.

Food spoilage is most commonly caused by three kinds of organisms: molds, yeasts, and bacteria. All three are heterotrophs (they must get food from some outside source). As we saw in the last chapter, not all molds spoil food as they digest it. But there are some varieties that seem to find old pieces of bread, or old oranges, and make them unfit to eat.

Yeasts are distant cousins of molds. They, too, are fungi and have no chlorophyll, so they must get food from outside sources. They usually exist as single cells, although there are a few varieties that form colonies with the threadlike connections you see in molds. The changes yeasts make in foods are not always undesirable. We would not have bread or wine without yeast, which makes bread dough rise and causes

grape juice to ferment. But there are varieties of yeast that spoil food. Fruit juices infected with some species of yeast can develop bubbles and an alcoholic smell as they ferment. Pickle juice can develop a film as yeast grows on its surface.

Bacteria are extremely tiny one-celled organisms. There are bacteria that change food in an appetizing manner: You'll remember that lactobacilli act on milk to produce yogurt and cheese. But there are many bacteria that can make food not only unappetizing but also poisonous. The horrible smells you associate with rotting food are often produced by bacteria.

The purpose of the various methods of food preservation is to limit or prevent the growth of food-spoiling organisms. But many of these methods, in their own special ways, also change the appearance or texture of the food being protected from spoilage. (There is no perfect way to preserve food so that it can be mistaken for fresh food, although we can come extremely close.) And many times the method of food preservation itself creates a new "dish" with a special flavor all its own, as you will see in the next experiment.

BEEF JERKY: DRYING AND CURING

One way of slowing down or stopping the growth of bacteria and food-destroying molds is to remove moisture, since moisture is essential for the growth of most microorganisms. When American Indians hung strips of buffalo meat in the sun and wind, they didn't know they were creating a less desirable environment for bacteria. But they did know that dried meat (which came to be called "jerky" after the Spanish word for this food, *charqui*) remained edible a lot longer than fresh meat. Also, it weighed less, making it easier to carry when they traveled over the range.

You could compare the rate of spoilage by leaving a piece of fresh beef and a piece of commercially prepared beef jerky at room temperature to see which spoils first. However, the results are quite predictable and completely inedible. So we will concentrate on exploring various techniques for preserving fresh beef by removing water. Is it better to dry beef in air or in the oven? Does salt have an effect on the drying process? Experiment and find out!

Materials and Equipment

> 1-pound flank steak
> sharp knife
> cutting board
> heavy bottle or mallet
> salt (coarse or Kosher salt if possible)
> dietetic or postal scale
> pan with rack (a cake rack, or use the rack in the
>   oven)
> string or long skewer
> paper and pencil

Procedure

Trim all fat from the steak. Cutting with the grain of the meat, make strips that are about 1 inch wide and ¼ inch thick. Since the steak is probably more than ¼ inch thick, you will have to split the steak through the thicker middle area by inserting the knife between the layers of muscle and cutting lengthwise. There should be eight to ten strips.

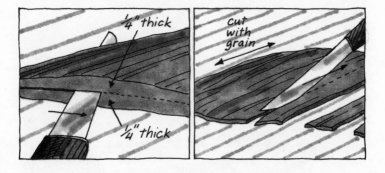

Lay the strips out on the cutting board and pound them with a heavy bottle (like a ketchup bottle) or a mallet until they are very thin. Divide the strips into two groups. Try to keep the two groups about equal to each other in the size and weight of strips. Sprinkle salt heavily on one group of strips. Pound the salt in. Turn the strips over and pound salt into the other side.

Divide the strips into four groups that will receive different treatment:

> Group 1: oven-dried, salted
> Group 2: oven-dried, unsalted
> Group 3: air-dried, salted
> Group 4: air-dried, unsalted

Weigh each strip carefully on a dietetic or postal scale. Record its weight. Note its position on the drying rack, if it is to be oven-dried, or its position on a line or skewer for air-drying.

You can hang strips for air-drying over a piece of string strung between two chairs. (We hung our strips by sticking a long shish kebab skewer through one end. The ends of the skewer were rested on the backs of two chairs, suspending the strips between them.) Hanging them near a radiator will shorten the drying time.

empty can holds door ajar

Place the pan with strips to be oven-dried in a *very* slow oven. It should be set at the lowest possible setting, about 150°F. Leave the oven door slightly ajar.

When dry, the jerky will be shriveled and dark. Our oven-dried beef jerky took 8½ hours to dry. The air-dried strips took about 36 hours.

Observations

The strips will feel lighter in weight when dry. Weigh each strip and calculate the percentage of weight loss using the following formula:

$$\text{Percentage of weight loss} = \frac{\text{fresh weight} - \text{dried weight}}{\text{fresh weight}} \times 100$$

After the oven-dried jerky cools, try breaking it. Try breaking an air-dried strip. Which treatment gives the crispest jerky? Which gives the toughest? Does salt have an effect on the drying process? Eating the jerky will give you some of the answers.

For Further Study

Pounding salt (or other spices) into meat is called dry-curing. Salt draws moisture out of meat; the water in the muscle cells flows out to the saltier area outside the cells. (We'll talk more about this in the *Beef "Tea"* experiment in Chapter 5.)

Try making beef jerky with a wet-curing or brine treatment. Soak the meat strips overnight in a mixture of ½ cup coarse salt in 2 cups water. Pat dry with a paper towel and use the air-drying or oven-drying procedure. Be sure to air- or oven-dry untreated strips simultaneously so you can compare results. Which is more effective, dry-curing or brine-curing, for the drying process?

SAUTÉED MUSHROOMS: DEHYDRATION AND RECONSTITUTION

Vegetables, like meat, can be dried as a means of preservation. Like all other plants, vegetables are made up of cells with a fairly rigid cell wall. The cell wall, in combination with water, gives structural support to the plant. When plant cells don't have enough water, they wilt. But the cell walls are not altered by the dehydration process, so when most of the water is removed, the lightweight remains are only slightly shriveled and have a rigid structure. Dried vegetables will resume their original shape if they are soaked in water. This process is called *reconstitution*.

The water content of mushrooms is extremely high. How high—that is, the percentage of water content—is one of the things you will find out in this experiment. You will dry mushrooms at home and compare them with commercially dehydrated mushrooms. The main difference between the commercial dehydration process and home dehydration is that industry dries vegetables in a partial vacuum (very low air pressure). This speeds up the rate at which water escapes into the atmosphere.

Materials and Equipment

5 or 6 large fresh mushrooms or 8 small ones
paper towels
dietetic or postal scale
paper and pencil
knife
broiler pan and rack
½-ounce container dehydrated mushrooms
small glass
water

Procedure

Wash the fresh mushrooms. Pat them dry with a paper towel. Weigh the whole batch together and record the weight. Slice them vertically into ⅛-inch slices. Spread the pieces on the rack in a broiler pan. Put in the oven at the lowest possible heat (about 150°F) for 4 to 6 hours. The mushrooms are dry when a slice can be broken cleanly.

Weigh your dried mushrooms and calculate the percentage of water lost:

$$\text{Percentage of water loss} = \frac{\text{fresh weight} - \text{dried weight}}{\text{fresh weight}} \times 100$$

Weigh the commercially dried mushrooms and record the weight. Put them in a small glass and cover with water. Let them soak for an hour. Drain and pat dry. Weigh again. Calculate the amount of water reabsorbed by the reconstituted mushrooms:

$$\text{Percentage of water reabsorbed} = \frac{\text{reconstituted weight} - \text{dried weight}}{\text{reconstituted weight}} \times 100$$

Observations

The moisture content of mushrooms is 90.4 percent. How close did your dehydration process come to removing this percentage of water? What percentage of water is reabsorbed by the commercially dried mushrooms? Reconstitute your home-dried mushrooms by the same procedure. Can you completely restore them to their original weight?

Theoretically, if completely dehydrated, mushrooms would lose more than 90 percent of their weight. But even if the weight loss is only 80 percent, the growth of microorganisms will be severely retarded, if not entirely prevented.

At the end of your experimenting, melt some butter in a small frying pan over medium heat and gently stir fry (sauté) the mushrooms until they are limp and heated through. Serve over steak, hamburger, or string beans.

For Further Study

Try this procedure on other dehydrated foods such as onions, fruits (apples work especially well), and green peas.

ZUCCHINI: FREEZING AND THAWING

Lower the temperature and you slow down the growth rate of microorganisms. That's the principle of refrigeration. But, as you undoubtedly know, food can and does spoil even under refrigeration if you keep it long enough. Freezing, however, stops microorganisms from growing. It doesn't kill them, so if thawing occurs, the microbes will start growing again. (That's why thawed food should be cooked and eaten as soon as possible.)

The main advantage of freezing is that it changes food from its fresh state less than any other method of food preservation. Even so, freezing can change the texture of foods, especially vegetables. This doesn't matter much if the vegetable is to be cooked, which would change its texture anyhow. But freezing vegetables like lettuce or tomatoes that are to be used raw in salads will give disappointing results. (You don't have to take our word for this—freeze some lettuce and see for yourself.)

Frozen food companies have spent a great deal of time and money developing ways to keep frozen vegetables as much like fresh as possible. In the next experiment you will investigate the difference between your home-freezing technique and that of commercial frozen food producers.

Materials and Equipment

1 package commercially frozen zucchini
1 small young zucchini squash
paper towels
knife
2 plastic sandwich bags with twist fasteners
freezer thermometer (optional)

Procedure

Put a package of commercially frozen zucchini into your freezer. Wash and pat dry the fresh zucchini squash. Slice into ½-inch slices. Put half of the slices into a plastic sandwich bag. Close tightly with a twist fastener. Put the bag into the freezer. Put the other half of the sliced zucchini into another plastic bag, fasten, and refrigerate. This is your control group, against which the effects of freezing will be compared. (The best experiments are "controlled" experiments—ones in which changes are introduced systematically, so that differences can be linked to the changes you make in the setup.)

The next day, take out the home-frozen zucchini and the package of commercially frozen zucchini. Allow them to thaw completely. This may take several hours. Compare the texture of the home-frozen squash with that of the commercially frozen and the unfrozen.

Observations

Which zucchini is firmest? Which is softest?

Frozen water has more volume (is less dense) than an equal weight of liquid water. If you've ever seen an aluminum can of soda stretched out of shape because it was left in the freezer to cool down quickly and then forgotten, you know what we mean. As the dried mushroom experiment showed, plant cells contain a great deal of water. When this water expands as it turns to ice, it can damage the cell walls, so the vegetable loses its crispness.

Commercially frozen zucchini is flash-frozen at about −20° F. How cold is your freezer? (You can measure with a freezer thermometer if you want.) When the freezing

process is slow, larger ice crystals form. Which zucchini must have had the largest ice crystals?

Put all the zucchini—including the refrigerated control—into a saucepan with about a cup of water. Bring to a boil and simmer for about 5 minutes. Drain and season with butter, salt, and pepper. Can you still tell the difference between fresh-cooked zucchini, home-frozen, and commercially frozen?

For Further Study

Check out the effect of freezing on meat. Cut a piece of steak in half and freeze one half. Refrigerate the other half. A day or so later, defrost the frozen steak. Compare it in appearance to the unfrozen half. Broil both and taste to see if there is a difference.

A food chemist at a meat-packing plant told us that animal cells are somewhat affected by ice crystals. The cells are enclosed in flexible protein membranes that can be broken down by sharp ice crystals, making the meat somewhat more tender. He also said that the difference was so slight he didn't think the average person would be able to detect it. Food chemists use a special instrument to measure the texture of meat. In *Science Experiments You Can Eat*, we developed a highly sophisticated procedure for measuring the tenderness of meat. It may be sensitive enough to detect a difference here.

CANNED FRUITS AND VEGETABLES: HIGH-ACID VERSUS LOW-ACID FOODS

Canned food was invented in 1809 when Napoleon Bonaparte held a contest to find a way to preserve food for his armies. The first "canned" goods were put in jars that were vacuum-sealed and then heated, killing all the microorganisms inside. (Of course, no one knew that this was what was happening. Louis Pasteur discovered microorganisms as the culprits in the spoilage of food and wine more than forty years later.) It has been said that if the canning process could have been kept a French national secret, Napoleon would have conquered the world. But by 1810, not only was the secret out, but an Englishman had improved the process, using "tins"—steel cans lined with tin—instead of jars.

Commercial canning today is one of the safest and longest-lasting ways of preserving food. Modern commercial canneries seal food in cans and pressure-cook them at about 250°F. So canned food is not only sterile, it is also cooked. Home canning is a project you might want to do with the cook in your house. However, the equipment needed, and the temperatures and pressures involved, make it too difficult and elaborate a procedure for this book. So we will restrict our experimenting to commercially canned food.

One of the factors that determines the temperature needed to kill bacteria is the amount of acid in food. Bacteria do not grow as well in high-acid foods (those with a sour taste), like grapefruit, as in low-acid foods, like green beans. In fact, one of the dangers in home canning of green beans and other low-acid foods is that incomplete sterilization will allow deadly botulinum bacteria to grow.

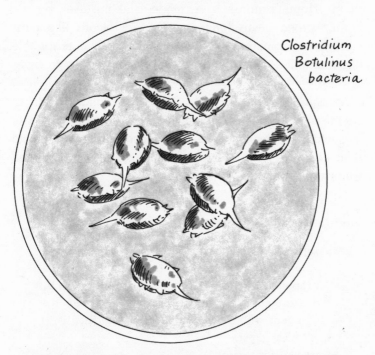

Clostridium
Botulinus
bacteria

These bacteria produce a substance that causes botulism, the most dreaded of all food poisoning. The poison causing botulism is so potent that the amount found in a single bean can kill an adult. The symptoms—vomiting, double vision, thirst, inability to swallow, thick saliva—appear within twenty-four hours after the affected food is eaten. Most cases (60 to 70 percent) are fatal, and recovery can take up to six months in those that are not. The reason botulism is such a danger in low-acid home canning is that the spores (the reproductive "seeds") of the bacteria are very common in gardens, and they can be very resistant to heat. The low-acid foods they are likely to grow in must be kept at boiling temperature for at least 20 minutes in order to kill them. Home canners have made fatal mistakes by not boiling green beans long enough. Acid foods like most varieties of tomatoes do not provide such a hospitable environment, so botulinum bacteria rarely grow in high-acid canned goods.

Measuring acidity is one of the most common jobs of chemists. It is fun, and it can have surprising results. Taste alone will not always tell you which food is more or less acid than another. In this experiment you'll measure canned fruits and vegetables for acidity.

Materials and Equipment

> a selection of the smallest cans of a few of the following: carrots, green beans, cherries, pineapple, apricots, peaches, pears, tomatoes, beets, asparagus, peas, corn, lima beans (look for the brands with the fewest added ingredients)
> small juice glasses
> teaspoons for stirring
> measuring spoons
> red cabbage indicator (see below)
> pencil and paper

To make red cabbage indicator you need:

    small red cabbage
    knife
    grater
    saucepan (not aluminum)
    strainer
    bowl
    measuring spoons
    2 juice glasses
    lemon juice
    baking soda

Cut the cabbage into quarters. Grate it section by section into a saucepan. Cover with water. Bring to a boil

and cook for about 5 minutes. Strain the water, which now contains red cabbage juice, into a bowl. (You can eat the red cabbage if you wish. Season with butter, salt, and pepper.)

Like litmus paper, red cabbage juice acts as an indicator. It changes color when it comes in contact with acids or their chemical opposite, bases. You can observe the color change by putting 2 tablespoons of red cabbage juice into each of two juice glasses. Add 1 teaspoon of lemon juice (a strong acid) to one glass and 1 teaspoon of baking soda (a base) to the other. Note the different color changes that result. The purple juice turns bright pink in acid and green in base.

Procedure

Most foods are on the acid side. Some are more acid than others. The method used to rank them is called *titration*. You will be counting the number of teaspoons of fruit or vegetable juice it takes to produce the color change that shows the presence of acid.

You'll need a small juice glass and a teaspoon for stirring for each canned item you are going to test. Put 2 tablespoons of red cabbage indicator in each glass. Add juice from the first canned food, 1 teaspoonful at a time. Stir each time you add juice. Keep a record of the number of teaspoons you need to get the color change to acid pink.

Observations

Rank your fruits and vegetables according to acidity. Check your results with the table here:

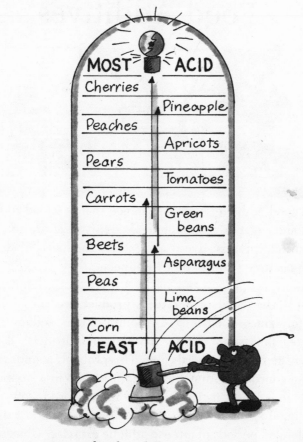

You may get results that differ from the above ranking. Differences can be caused by the presence of flavorings and other juices added during the canning process. Check labels to see if you are getting the most simply processed product with the fewest additives.

4

Food Additives

A food additive is any substance that is added to food. Salt and sugar are common food additives, as are coloring, flavoring, preservatives, and other chemicals that food manufacturers add to their products.

Many people are put off by the idea of "chemicals in food." The label of a typical product reads as follows: Water, glucose, citric acid, sodium citrate, sodium phosphate, potassium citrate, natural and artificial flavors, ester, gum, and artificial color. This probably sounds to you like a concoction some fiend might mix up in a laboratory. But in reality it is a lemon-lime-flavored soft drink designed specifically to replace the body salts lost during prolonged periods of intense athletic exercise. Glucose is a simple sugar (sucrose is the technical name for the variety of sugar you use at your table); citric acid and sodium citrate are the distinctive substances that make lemons and limes taste like lemons and limes. The truth is that all food is made up of chemicals. Natural substances like steak, as well as man-made ones like the drink referred to above, can be described by chemical formulas. Some chemical substances are indeed harmful, but a person who refused to consume any chemicals would find nothing to eat.

The things we eat can be divided into natural and artificial (man-made) substances. Some people feel that only natural foods are healthful and that all artificial ingredients are to be avoided. But many natural chemicals, found in plants and animals, are harmful when eaten, and some laboratory-made substances increase the nutritional value of food. Other chemicals have natural and artificial forms that are exactly alike: vitamin C is vitamin C, whether it comes from a test tube or from an orange. Like "chemical," "artificial" doesn't necessarily mean "not fit to eat."

Food additives are used for many reasons. We add sugar and salt and other flavorings to foods we prepare at home to make them taste better. Food manufacturers have developed a range of additives that bleach, stabilize, tenderize, thicken, harden, clarify, fortify, keep dry, keep moist, keep crisp, keep firm, or improve the appearance of their products. Additives can make food more convenient or nutritious, give it a longer shelf life, and make it more attractive to the consumer, thus increasing the sales and profits of the manufacturers.

Food additives are presently the center of a storm of controversy. Food manufacturers have been known to use additives that had not been proved safe; some substances in common use have been proved unsafe, or potentially unsafe, and have been taken off the market. Many people feel there is a risk involved in eating food to which anything has been added. For people with allergies or other special sensitivities, this may often be true. But food additives are now regulated by the Food and Drug Administration of the federal government, and new additives are subjected to extensive testing before they can be placed on the market. The FDA has compiled a list of those Generally Regarded As Safe (the GRAS List). For most people, the chances of developing serious side effects from the long-term use of presently approved food additives are very slim.

The experiments in this chapter will familiarize you with a few food additives and show how they are used in the production and processing of food.

Vitamin C Hunt

It is perhaps fitting to begin our exploration of food additives by taking a close look at a substance that is both natural- and laboratory-made, is found in many foods, and is added to many others—namely, vitamin C.

The story of vitamin C began hundreds of years ago, before the beginning of modern chemistry. Many people suffered from a disease called "spring sickness" or scorbutus. The symptoms were bleeding gums, loose teeth, aching joints, red spots on the skin, and decayed flesh.

Today, this disease is known as scurvy. Sailors were particularly susceptible to scurvy. In the last part of the eighteenth century, sauerkraut and citrus fruit were taken along on English ships bound on long voyages. Miraculously, these foods eliminated the disease. (Can you guess why British sailors are called "limeys"?) But it wasn't until 1932 that the chemical in these foods, named *ascorbic* (meaning "no scurvy") *acid*, was purified in a laboratory.

Ascorbic acid, or vitamin C, is now known to be extremely important for the body's manufacturing of *collagen*, the protein responsible for keeping cells, muscles, and bones connected to each other. A lack of collagen causes the cells of the tiniest blood vessels to separate and allows blood to leak into tissues, resulting in the bleeding gums and red splotches characteristic of scurvy.

The experiment you'll perform is a chemical test for vitamin C that can tell you whether this wondrous chemical can be found in any food you choose to check out.

Materials and Equipment

    cornstarch
    measuring spoons
    saucepan (stainless steel or enamel, not aluminum)
    measuring cup
    knife
    spoons for stirring
    jars for stock starch solution and vitamin C test
        solution
    iodine
    250-milligram vitamin C tablet
    small juice glasses
    medicine dropper or straws that can be used as
        droppers
    samples of various foods, such as: tomato juice,
        orange juice, cabbage juice, pickle juice, etc.

Procedure

This procedure tells you more than if vitamin C is present or not; it gives you an idea of how much is present. So it is very important to measure all ingredients carefully.

Put ½ teaspoon cornstarch in a saucepan with 1 cup of water. (Make sure you use a level teaspoon: pass the back of a knife over the spoon, leveling off the cornstarch.) Place the pan over low heat and stir until the starch is completely dissolved. Pour into a jar and allow to cool. This is your stock starch solution. It may be kept for several days in the refrigerator. However, the best results are obtained when the starch solution is fresh.

Now make up your vitamin C test solution. Put 1 teaspoon of the stock starch solution in a jar with 1 cup of water and 4 drops of iodine. The solution will have a blue color because iodine combines with the starch to form a colored molecule.

Note: *None of the test solutions is edible. Iodine is poison! The only thing you can eat in this experiment is the food you take the test samples from, not the samples themselves.**

First, do a positive test for vitamin C. Dissolve a 250-milligram tablet of vitamin C in 1 cup of water. Put 2 tablespoons of your starch-and-iodine test solution in a small glass. Add a drop of vitamin C solution and stir. What happens to the blue iodine-starch mixture?

Your vitamin C hunt can give you a relative check on how much vitamin C is present in a sample. Add your food sample drop by drop to 2 tablespoons of vitamin C test solution in a small glass. You can add drops with a medicine dropper or with a plastic straw used as a pipette. Simply draw up a sample of juice into the straw with your mouth (as if you were going to drink through the straw, only don't suck the liquid all the way to your mouth). Cover the top of the straw with your finger. This holds the juice in the

---

*Iodine in very, very small amounts is essential for health. A person whose diet does not include trace amounts of iodine can develop an enlarged thyroid gland. For this reason, a very small proportion of iodine is added to table salt, which is sold as "iodized salt." This should not be confused with the iodine that is used for antiseptic purposes, which must not be eaten.

straw. If you carefully raise your fingertip by slightly bending the first joint, you can let out the juice drop by drop. Pipetting takes practice, so don't try this in an actual experiment until you can control the flow of drops. The number of drops needed to make the test solution colorless is a measure of the amount of vitamin C present in the sample. Be sure to stir the solution or swirl the glass with the addition of each drop. Use a clean straw for each food sample, or rinse the medicine dropper between tests.

Observations

Check citrus fruit juices, sauerkraut juice, other fruit juices, tomato juice, and pickle juice. Check other foods. Vitamin C dissolves in water, so solid foods can be soaked in water to remove the vitamin, which can then be checked for with the test solution. Make up more test solution as needed.

For Further Study

See what effects heat has on vitamin C. Boil a sample of pure vitamin C solution and see if you still get positive results. Allow vitamin C solution to stand in a jar in sunlight for a week. Then check against a fresh solution to see if light destroys vitamin C.

What do your results show about the best way to treat orange juice? Dairy cases contain light similar to sunlight. Should you buy orange juice in a waxed carton or in a transparent bottle? Why?

VITAMIN C VERSUS OXYGEN

Fruit and meat both change color on exposure to air. Vitamin C is often added to foods to interfere with such color changes. In this experiment you find out just how vitamin C plays a role in changing a natural course of events.

Materials and Equipment

> 250-milligram vitamin C tablet
> measuring cup
> spoon for stirring
> peach
> knife
> 2 plates
> pastry brush
> water
> ½ pound fresh ground beef

Procedure

Dissolve a vitamin C tablet in 1 cup of water. Peel and slice a peach. Put half the slices on one plate and half on

slice peel away from fingers

another plate. With a pastry brush, paint one group of slices liberally with water. This is your control group. Paint the other group liberally with vitamin C solution.

The ground beef should look bright red on the surface but be dark inside when you break off a piece. Can you think of a reason why exposure to air might explain this difference? Divide the meat in half. Paint the dark surface of one portion of the meat with water and the dark surface of the other with vitamin C solution. Let the meat stand exposed to the air for up to an hour, or until one sample turns red.

Observations

How does vitamin C affect the browning reaction of fruit? Lemon juice contains vitamin C. Why do you think cooks often squeeze lemon juice on sliced apples that are waiting to be put into apple pie?

Would a butcher add vitamin C to chopped meat? Why not?

When oxygen combines chemically with foods, the results are sometimes considered unappetizing and sometimes desirable. For example, freshly ground beef is bright red throughout, because the oxygen-carrying pigment in the meat combines with oxygen in the air. As the meat stands, the inside becomes dark due to lack of contact with oxygen. Meat that has been standing for a while eventually loses its ability to combine with oxygen. The redness of the outside meat is therefore an indication of how fresh it is, so this reaction can be considered desirable.

Cut fruit, on the other hand, reacts with oxygen by turning brown. Sliced, frozen peaches are not at all appealing if they are not treated with an antioxidant—a food additive that prevents oxygen from combining with the fruit and therefore prevents browning. Vitamin C is such an antioxidant. It is often added to foods to prevent undesirable reactions with oxygen.

All the peaches in this experiment are edible. And you can make hamburgers out of the ground beef.

For Further Study

Check out the effect of vitamin C on other fruits and vegetables, such as potatoes, apples, and bananas.

Vitamin C supposedly reacts with the protein in bread dough, making it lighter and easier to knead. Design an experiment to test this, making bread with and without vitamin C. Dissolve about 1,000 milligrams in the water for 1 loaf as a start. You may want to experiment with the quantities. (Adding vitamin C to bread dough does not increase the nutritional value of the bread. Baking destroys the vitamin.)

VITAMIN E AS AN ANTIOXIDANT

First, we must admit that in this experiment there is nothing you can really eat, except the lemon. However, it does demonstrate an important use of vitamin E as a preservative. In this experiment you smell the effects of vitamin E on lemon oil.

Materials and Equipment

> sharp knife
> lemon
> coffee filter paper or paper towel
> cutting board
> hammer
> vitamin E capsule

Procedure

Slice several thin pieces of lemon rind off the lemon. Put one piece skin side down on a piece of filter paper resting on the cutting board. Hammer the rind so that the oil in the skin is pounded into the filter paper. (Some water will

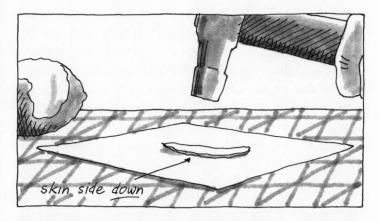

skin side down

also be extracted, but this will soon evaporate.) Prepare another piece of filter paper with hammer-extracted lemon oil. Note the smell of the freshly drawn oil.

Cut the vitamin E capsule open. Spread vitamin E oil over one of the lemon oil samples. Leave the papers exposed to the air for several hours.

spread vitamin E oil

Observations

Smell both papers periodically. You will notice that vitamin E has a sweet odor that fails to mask the smell of the lemon oil. The untreated lemon oil soon develops a rancid smell. What happens to the treated lemon oil?

Again, oxygen is the bad guy, the spoiler of food. When oxygen combines with certain oils or fats, they become rancid. This condition is easily detected by the distinctive odor of rancidity, vaguely resembling turpentine. Obviously vegetable oil manufacturers want to retard this process in their products, so they add antioxidants. Vitamin C won't do in this case because it is water-soluble and won't dissolve in fats. But vitamin E is fat-soluble and does the job quite nicely.

For Further Study

Repeat this procedure to see if vitamin E retards the spoilage of butter. Spread butter on two pieces of filter paper and rub vitamin E into one. Or you can prepare your own butter by shaking heavy cream in a jar. Divide the cream into two samples, adding vitamin E to one. Shake until butter forms. The vitamin E will remain in the butter, as it is fat-soluble. The buttermilk can be discarded. Leave the pats of butter in the refrigerator uncovered. Smell over a period of several days. Does vitamin E retard rancidity?

Can you explain why vitamin E will not be as effective as vitamin C in preventing fruit from browning?

Chocolate Pudding: Carrageenan Stabilization

Carrageenan is a carbohydrate extracted from sun-dried Irish moss seaweed. Cooks in Ireland and France began using it hundreds of years ago as an ingredient in milk puddings. Carrageenan is the most effective stabilizer for milk-based foods because of the unique way in which its molecules combine with milk protein.

In this experiment you see the effect of carrageenan in chocolate pudding. Since pudding mixes all contain carrageenan, you'll need to make pudding from scratch in order to observe the effect.

Carrageen
seaweed

Materials and Equipment

    bakers' (unsweetened) chocolate
    double boiler
    spoons for stirring
    measuring cup
    sugar
    16 ounces evaporated milk (check the label to make
        sure it contains carrageenan)
    salt
    measuring spoons
    knife for making level measures
    cornstarch
    vanilla extract
    2 medium-size bowls
    fresh milk

Procedure

Put 1 ounce (a square) of chocolate in the top of a double boiler over boiling water and heat until melted. Slowly stir in ½ cup sugar, 1¾ cups evaporated milk with carrageenan, and a dash of salt. While this mixture is heating, dissolve 3 level tablespoons cornstarch in ¼ cup evaporated milk. Slowly add this mixture to the hot milk mixture,

stirring constantly. Continue heating and stirring the pudding until it is thickened and does not taste of raw cornstarch (about 10 minutes).

Remove the pudding from the heat. When it is slightly cool, stir in 1 teaspoon vanilla extract. Pour into a bowl. Allow pudding to cool to room temperature before refrigerating.

Repeat the recipe, substituting fresh milk for evaporated. This pudding, your control, will not have carrageenan in it.

Observations

Which pudding forms a skin? Allow the puddings to remain in the refrigerator for at least a day before eating. As they age, which one "weeps" more (develops more watery fluid around the edges)? How would you describe the stabilizing effects of carrageenan?

Carrageenan combines with milk protein in a way that prevents butterfat from separating from the watery part of milk. For this reason, puddings that contain carrageenan should not "weep," while those made without carrageenan weep as they age. The skin that forms on the control pudding is coagulated milk protein. Because carrageenan binds this protein, keeping the pudding smooth, skin doesn't form on the experimental pudding.

Carrageenan is also used to add "body" to soft drinks, to prevent large ice crystals from forming in ice cream, and to prevent the oil in whipped topping from separating out. And it is used to prevent the butterfat in evaporated milk from separating out. Why does the pudding made with evaporated milk taste distinctively different from that made with fresh milk?

WHIPPED TOPPING: ACID-STABILIZED FOAM

A whipped topping that stays whipped and stiff for a while has obvious advantages. In this experiment you investigate the effect of adding an acid to a whipped dessert topping made from evaporated milk. And yes, it has fewer calories than whipped cream, which will please any family members who are weight-conscious.

Materials and Equipment

1 can evaporated milk
measuring cup
2 bowls
egg beater or electric beater
spoon for stirring
measuring spoons
sugar
lemon juice
eggs
cream of tartar

Procedure

Put half a can of evaporated milk in each bowl. Put both bowls in the freezer. After about an hour or two, ice crystals should start appearing in the bowls. This is the sign it's time to start experimenting.

Whip the contents of one bowl with an egg beater or with an electric beater until the milk stands in stiff peaks. This takes considerably more time than preparing whipped cream or beating egg whites, so stay with it. Gently stir 1 tablespoon of sugar into the topping and refrigerate.

Now repeat the procedure with the contents of the other bowl. When the second mixture begins to get thick, add 1 tablespoon of lemon juice and continue beating until the mixture stands in stiff peaks. Add 1 tablespoon sugar, as you did with the other sample, and refrigerate. Every half hour check your foams by gently spooning up a peak. Watch to see how long they hold their shape.

Observations

Which foam holds a peak longer? Which foam separates into a liquid sooner? How much difference does the acid seem to make?

Acids react with proteins to alter the structure of the protein molecules. This process is called *denaturation*. You can see acid denature milk proteins if you squeeze lemon juice into milk. Clumping is one evidence of denaturation. An acid added to proteins being mechanically denatured by whipping should strengthen the altered chemical structure.

A variation on this experiment is to repeat the procedure with egg whites. Beat two batches of egg whites until stiff. In one batch, add ¼ teaspoon cream of tartar (a common household acid) for every egg white you use. Leave the control batch untreated. Keep the beaten egg whites at room temperature while watching for the effects of the acid.

When you've finished the experiment, make a meringue: Combine both bowls of egg whites and slowly beat in ¼ cup sugar for each egg white until stiff and thick. Bake in a greased pie pan in a slow oven (200°F) until dry, about 1 hour. Turn the oven off and let the meringue sit until cool. Fill with fruit, such as defrosted strawberries, and use your whipped topping.

Food Coloring: Natural Versus Artificial

If you don't think the color of food is important, try serving up blue mashed potatoes or green scrambled eggs. To get these unusual results, just add a few drops of the food coloring you can buy in any supermarket. The odds are high that perfectly nutritious but unexpectedly colored food will go uneaten.

Food processing and the manufacturing of convenience foods can produce results that are delicious but that look very unappetizing. Often most of the natural color is lost in the preparation. For this reason food manufacturers add coloring to foods to restore them to their original and expected color. Red food dyes are added to frankfurters that would otherwise look gray. Ripe oranges from Florida that have green or spotted skins may have these defects masked by orange dye. Without food coloring, soft drinks, ice cream, pistachio nuts, candy, baked goods, pet foods, sausage, and breakfast cereals would be much less colorful and much less appealing. Of course, it is entirely possible that in time people would adjust to the natural colors of food. But no food manufacturer is going to risk sales during the time needed for such a period of adjustment. Color is too important to profits. So food coloring is one of the most widely used of all food additives.

There are, of course, many natural food colorings that have been used for centuries. These include paprika, turmeric, and saffron, along with red pigments found in beets, yellow pigments in carrots and pumpkins, and greens in leaves. Unfortunately, most natural colors fade, are expensive to produce, and have low coloring power. In the last half of the nineteenth century, chemists discovered how to make intensely colored dyes from coal tar. Now coal tar is a dangerously inedible substance. But the FDA (Food and Drug Administration) has certified four food colors— one blue, two reds, and one yellow—that seem to be quite harmless. Some people feel that the studies of these food colors do not meet rigorous scientific standards, but in the fifty-plus years these particular dyes have been in use no evidence has overturned the FDA certification.

There are laws regulating the use of these approved food colors. Artificial coloring may not be used to mask food that is unhealthy. It cannot be used to make unripe fruit ripe, or make tainted meat seem fresh, or make noodles appear to contain eggs when they don't. And products containing artificial coloring must state this on the label. However, you don't have to read the label to see if a food contains artificial color. This experiment is a procedure for detecting coal tar dyes in food.

Materials and Equipment

> samples of colored juices and waters including, for
> instance: beet juice, tomato juice, sodas, teas,
> maraschino cherries, grenadine, fruit syrups,
> jellies, water from canned and cooked vegeta-
> bles, powders like paprika, saffron, or turmeric
> mixed into ½ cup water, and anything else you
> can think of
>
> 2-cup saucepan (not aluminum)
> vinegar
> white wool yarn (make sure you don't use acrylic)
> scissors

Procedure

Put a sample of the colored liquid in a saucepan with a
few drops of vinegar and a 3-inch piece of white yarn. Heat
to boiling. Lift out the yarn and rinse it in cold water. If the
wool retains the color of the liquid, the substance contains
artificial coloring made from coal tar.

Observations

The protein in wool reacts with the coal tar dyes in an acid environment so that *chemical bonding* occurs. The molecules interlock, forming a new stable substance. Natural dyes do not form this bond with wool, so the yarn will become white again when washed.

Check your results against labels. You should get positive results when the use of FDA-certified color is indicated on labels.

Naturally you can eat the juice you heat with the wool if you want. We don't recommend eating the wool. And we make no claims for the flavor.

MSG: A FLAVOR ENHANCER

Monosodium glutamate, or MSG, was originally discovered in Japanese seaweed. Cooks found that certain soups containing this seaweed were tastier than soups cooked with seaweed that did not contain MSG. The chemical was isolated from the seaweed as pure white crystals in 1908, and by 1910 it was sold commercially. MSG is used by cooks in much the same way as salt—sometimes food is cooked with it and sometimes it is sprinkled over food after it is cooked. By itself, MSG has a pleasant, mild flavor somewhere between sweet and salty, and produces a "mouth feel." It cannot be tasted in food, but it does have an effect on the natural flavors of foods.

However, you don't have to take our word for it or even the word of the manufacturer. The idea of this experiment is to see for yourself why MSG is called a "flavor enhancer" and to see if it has an effect on all foods.

Note: Some people have an unpleasant reaction to MSG—a burning feeling in the back of the neck and forearms, a tightness in the chest, and a headache. Since MSG is used liberally in much Chinese food, this reaction is called the "Chinese restaurant syndrome." If you or any members of your family suffer some of these reactions after eating Chinese food, don't do this experiment. However, studies of the Chinese restaurant syndrome have demonstrated that it is not permanently dangerous to health, though temporarily it can be very annoying. Because MSG is found naturally in many foods, and because it is not dangerous to health, it is on the GRAS ("Generally Regarded As Safe") list.

Materials and Equipment

> family dinner (see below)
> masking tape for labels
> marking pencil
> monosodium glutamate (Ac´cent is one brand name)
> paper and pencils

Procedure

You will need the cooperation of the cook in your house for this experiment, as it will involve your entire family and the main meal of the day. (In fact, this experiment will give more valid results if it is repeated for several days.)

Divide each dish you are having for dinner into two serving bowls. Label one bowl A and the other B. Sprinkle one of the samples with MSG and leave the other untreated. Use about half a teaspoon on each dish. Make sure you keep a record of which dish has been treated and vary your treatment patterns in a random way so that both A and B dishes are treated. For example, your list of treated dishes could read: salad A, mashed potatoes B, hamburgers B . . .

Before dinner, make up questionnaires on sheets of paper for the members of your family. They should look like this:

Comments:	A	B
soup		
salad		
meat		
gravy		
mashed potatoes		
peas		
carrots		
pudding		

Tell your family to take a sample from each dish, remembering if it is an A or B dish. They are to taste a sample, take a sip of water, then taste the other sample. Then they should record on their questionnaires which sample is tastier, A or B, along with their comments about the taste. Ask them to describe any differences they detect. It is important that they not discuss the dishes or flavors with one another. And it is also a good idea for them not to know you have treated half the dishes with MSG.

Repeat the experiment for several nights if possible.

Observations

Does MSG make a difference? Do people pick the dishes containing MSG as tastier? Are the flavors of some kinds of foods, such as meats, enhanced more than others? What words did your family use to describe differences in taste? Why is it important that they not know what the experiment is about? Did your knowledge of which dishes contained MSG affect your judgment?

5

Flavorings and Extracts

Some of the chemicals in food have the unique ability to stimulate specialized nerves in our tongues and noses to give the sensation of taste. Usually these flavorful substances make up an exceedingly small proportion of any given food, measured in parts per million. Strong stuff, indeed! In Chapter 6 we'll explore the way our nerve cells and brains react to some of the chemicals and translate their messages into different sensations of taste. In this chapter we'll look at some of the properties of flavoring from the chemical point of view.

A "Tea" Party: Solubility of Flavors

Many flavorful chemicals are soluble—can be dissolved—in water. The ease with which this occurs depends, in part, on the structure of the chemical's molecules. Some flavorful chemicals dissolve more completely in another solvent, such as alcohol, than in water. Vanilla extract, for example, is made up of alcohol-soluble chemicals extracted from vanilla beans. But there are many chemicals that dissolve easily in water. Chemists call a hot-water solution an *infusion*. Two common infusions prepared in kitchens are coffee and tea.

In this experiment you will discover some of the many flavors that make delicious drinks and the best conditions for extracting them.

Materials and Equipment

> teaspoons
> tea ball or tea strainer
> spices, whole or ground: allspice (dried berries), anise (seeds), cinnamon (bark), cloves (buds), fennel (seeds), and ground nutmeg (seed), and/or herbs, whole leaves: basil, marjoram, mint, oregano, rosemary, sage
> teakettle
> boiling water
> teacups
> sugar
> paper and pencil

Procedure

Put about ¼ teaspoon of an herb or spice in the tea ball or strainer for each cup of "tea." Pour freshly boiling water into a teacup and let the herb or spice steep in it for 3 or 4 minutes. Remove the tea ball or strainer and taste. Add sugar if you wish.

Try to write a description of the taste. You can begin to

appreciate the difficulty of trying to measure flavor. (We will talk about this in greater depth in Chapter 6.)

Here are some suggestions for words to describe the flavors you are tasting: bitter, astringent (mouth-puckering), pungent (strong), tangy, biting, sour, tart.

After you get a sense of the flavors of single herbs and spices, make combinations. We thought tea made with cloves, nutmeg, and cinnamon was delicious. You can also try adding a small amount of orange rind.

For Further Study

The temperature of the water is another factor that determines how readily a soluble chemical will enter into solution. Experiment with the effect of temperature on preparing a flavored extract. Use the tea ball and spices or herbs. Try hot water, cold water, and boiling water. Allow all samples to cool to room temperature and then taste. What effect does water temperature have on the preparation of an infusion? In general, most chemicals dissolve more readily in hot water than in cold.

Tea to a T: Temperature for the "Perfect" Infusion

Some tea drinkers are very fussy about the way their tea is brewed. Their sense of taste, when it comes to tea, has been developed to a highly discriminating degree. And such tea appreciators agree on two things: that the water should just reach a rolling boil before it is used for brewing, and that the pot or cups should be preheated. In this experiment you will determine for yourself whether temperature and length of boiling have an effect on the taste of tea.

Materials and Equipment

> teakettle
> small saucepan
> 3 teacups
> 3 tea bags
> 3 teaspoons
> watch, clock, or kitchen timer
> candy thermometer (optional)

Procedure

Put water in the teakettle and heat it on the stove. This water will be used to heat up the teacups. A few minutes after you put on the kettle, put about a quart of water in the saucepan and put it on to boil also. This water will be used to make tea. Set out the 3 teacups with a tea bag beside (not in) each one.

The important part of this procedure is to time everything around the boiling of the water in the saucepan. Ideally, the water in the teakettle should come to a full boil shortly before bubbles start rising to the surface in the saucepan. When the water in the kettle boils, use it to fill the three cups to heat them. Now carefully watch the water in the saucepan. As soon as boiling starts—when small bubbles break free from the bottom of the pan—quickly pour the hot water from one of the cups into the sink. Pour the barely boiling water from the pan into the cup and put in a tea bag. Let it steep for 4 minutes.

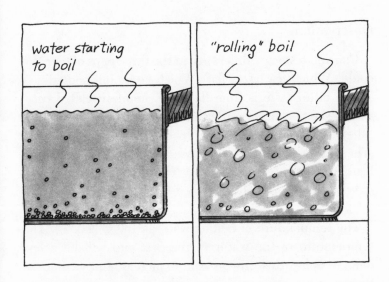

Meanwhile, immediately put the pan with the remaining water back on the fire. Again watch it carefully. As soon as it reaches a rolling boil (where large bubbles create a violently moving surface), pour the hot water out of the second cup, pour in the boiling water, and put in a fresh tea bag. Again, let it steep for 4 minutes. Put the pan back on the fire and let it continue to boil for 4 minutes. Then prepare the last cup of tea in the same manner. It's important that you time the steeping of the tea so that variation in the strength and quality of the brew does not occur because the tea bags have been sitting in the cups for different lengths of time.

Taste the three cups of tea, rinsing out your mouth with cool water between tastes. (This technique was developed by professional tea tasters.) Roll the tea around in your mouth before swallowing.

Observations

Can you taste any difference in the three cups of tea? We could. Which tea tastes flat? Which tastes full-bodied?

The bitter taste is from flavorful chemicals called *catechins*. The puckering sensation in the skin of your mouth is called *astringency;* it's caused by chemicals called *tannins*. (These same chemicals are used for curing or tanning leather.) Both catechins and tannins should be well developed (completely extracted from the leaves) in well-made tea.

The temperature of boiling water is 100°C (212°F). The temperature of the water in the first cup will be a few degrees below this. (If you want to increase the accuracy of this experiment, use a candy thermometer to measure water temperature.) The water in the second and third cups will be at boiling temperature. However, the water that has been boiled those extra minutes will have lost its dissolved gases. Tea lovers claim that if tea leaves are added to water that is not hot enough, the tea will not develop its full flavor. And if the water has been boiled too long, the tea leaves don't open and the tea tastes flat. Do you agree?

Tea lovers claim that the kind of water you use also affects the flavor of tea. Compare tea made with tap water to tea made with bottled spring water from various places.

For Further Study

There is only one kind of tea plant. There are, however, many different varieties of tea. There are a number of factors causing this great variety: different conditions where tea is grown, different ways tea leaves are processed, and different herbs and spices which may be mixed with tea. Green tea is made up of tea leaves that are dried right after picking. Black tea is made up of tea leaves that are allowed to ferment. Microorganisms change the color and develop the full flavor of black tea. Oolong tea is partially fermented.

You might want to compare the flavors of green, oolong, and black teas to see how the process of fermenting affects the taste. To make this experiment as controlled as possible, try to get teas that have been grown in the same part of the world.

Beef "Tea": Extraction of Water-Soluble Meat Chemicals

It just so happens that the main flavorful chemicals in meat are water-soluble. They can be found in the pan drippings from roast meat that are used to make gravy. The next time you have a roast for dinner, look for a brownish, congealed substance in the bottom of the pan or attached to the underside of the roast.

Here's how it forms: As meat cooks, the structural protein of the meat loses its ability to hold moisture. Water oozes out of the meat, carrying water-soluble chemicals with it. If you taste the pan drippings, you will find they have a very strong meat flavor.

In this experiment you make use of two very common chemistry lab techniques—use of the boiling water bath and filtration. In kitchens, the usual boiling water bath is a pot called a double boiler. The purpose of a boiling water bath is to heat the contents at the constant temperature of boiling water. Filtration is often used in kitchens to make coffee.

You will also see how salt changes the quality of the extract.

Materials and Equipment

1 pound *very* lean ground beef
4 1½- to 2-cup jars with screw tops (peanut butter jars
    are great)
measuring cup
fork for stirring
measuring spoons
salt
adhesive label and pen
large soup pot
pot holders
funnel (or top of filter coffee maker)
coffee filter paper

Procedure

When you buy the beef for this experiment, pick out a
piece of lean beef, such as chuck London broil, and have
the butcher trim all the fat off and grind it for you. It's very
important that the meat be as free of fat as possible.

Divide the meat in half and place each half in a jar. Add
½ cup water to each jar and stir, breaking up the meat. Add
½ teaspoon salt to one of the jars. Screw on the tops tightly.
Label the jar that has salt in it.

Put both jars in the soup pot and fill with water to near the tops of the jars. Put the pot on the stove and bring the water to a boil. (Since boiling water is at 100°C [212°F], you know that the contents of the jars will never get any hotter than this.) Let the jars sit in the boiling water bath for 2 hours. Check the water level occasionally and replace water when the level gets lower.

Remove the jars (use pot holders) and let them cool. The water surrounding the meat will have a slightly yellowish color. The next step is to separate the broth, or *filtrate*, from the meat. Set up the funnel in another jar and line it with a filter paper. Pour the contents of one jar into the filter. Let the liquid drip through. Repeat the filtering procedure with a clean jar and a new piece of filter paper for the contents of the other jar. Set the meat samples aside.

Observations

Taste the filtrates. Which tastes more flavorful? Add ½ teaspoon salt to the unsalted filtrate. Does it now taste the same as the other, or does one extract have a stronger flavor? Does salted water draw out more flavorful chemicals than unsalted? Taste the meat that is left behind. How can you explain its taste? Does the filter paper give a clue to the size of the particles of the flavorful chemicals in the filtrate? Scientists often use filters with different size holes or "pores" (sometimes submicroscopic) as a measure of the size of particles.

The broths can be used as bouillon. Heat and add lemon juice to serve. You can put the meat in spaghetti sauce or feed it to your dog.

ALL KINDS OF EXTRACTS: DISTILLATION

The sense of smell is crucial to the overall sense of taste. And smell alone can tell you a great deal about what's cooking. Most aromas are due to volatile chemicals—that is, chemicals that evaporate into the air. Many volatile chemicals in food evaporate at temperatures lower than 100°C, the temperature of boiling water. And because they have lower boiling points we can collect these volatile substances by a process called *distillation*.

No chemistry lab is complete without a distillation apparatus. Laboratory glassware for distillation has been especially designed for this purpose. It consists of a vessel for boiling and a condenser. Steam passes through the condenser and is rapidly cooled by cold water running through an outside tube. The steam returns to its liquid state with the volatile chemicals in it.

In this experiment you assemble your own distillation apparatus so that you can make many kinds of *distillates* (condensed water containing the volatile components) in your own kitchen.

Materials and Equipment

Note: Creativity in this experiment comes in collecting and assembling your equipment from what you have on hand. The only rule here is to improvise.

> 3-quart stainless steel, enamel, or glass saucepan (not cast iron or aluminum)
> small curved saucer or ashtray to be used as a collecting dish
> clean brick or small jar that will be a stand for the collecting dish (we used a jar that had contained marinated artichoke hearts, and filled it with water so it would rest on the bottom of the saucepan and not float away)
> water
> cinnamon or any other spice
> heat-resistant glass bowl that fits into the saucepan, to be filled with ice water

Procedure

Put the saucepan on a stove burner. Rest the shallow collecting dish on the water-filled jar or brick in the center of the saucepan. Mix about 2 cups of water with cinnamon or some other herb or spice. We used about 3 teaspoons of

cinnamon. When heated, this makes an infusion from which you will distill the volatile chemicals. Pour it into the saucepan.

Cover the assemblage with the heatproof glass bowl containing ice water, and turn on a medium flame.

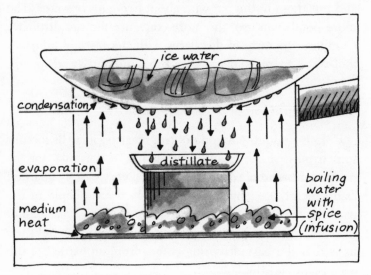

Observations

Here's how your distillation apparatus works: When the water in the saucepan boils, water vapor and volatile chemicals rise from its surface. When these gaseous materials strike the cold surface of the glass bowl, they condense, or return to a liquid state. (Temperature is one of the important factors that determines when a particular substance changes from a liquid to a gas and vice versa.) The condensed liquid (the distillate) runs down the bottom of the bowl and drips into the shallow dish in the center of the saucepan.

You can use your distillation apparatus to make all kinds of distillates. Try all the herbs and spices in your spice rack. Try fresh and dried fruits. You can keep your extracts in small jars in the refrigerator and use them in cooking. You can also make rosewater. Wash the petals of a rose or two and put them in the pot with about two cups of water. The more petals you use, the more concentrated the distillate. Compare the taste of distillates with the taste of infusions (hot-water extracts) made from the same herbs and spices.

SYNTHETIC COLA

Cola is undoubtedly one of the most popular flavors for soft drinks. Each manufacturer has a formula for its particular brand of cola syrup that is a very closely guarded trade secret. Legend has it that only three people in the world know the recipe for the syrup of Coca-Cola, one of the most popular brands. All any manufacturer would tell us is that the basic flavoring comes from an extract of the coca plant and the kola nut.

coca leaves

kola nut

One of our sources said that Coca-Cola contains only traces of extracts from the coca plant and kola nut, and that it is actually a concoction that may include cinnamon, vanilla, lime juice, and sugar. There is a report that when Cubans couldn't get Coca-Cola they figured out how to make their own. In this experiment you will try to crack one of the most closely guarded of all trade secrets—the formula for Coke.

Materials and Equipment

sugar
vanilla extract
powdered cinnamon
bottled sweetened lime juice
club soda
measuring cup and spoons
ice
glasses
two or three different brands of cola (not diet)
a blindfold
a willing friend

Procedure

We used the following proportions in mixing our synthetic cola:

1 tablespoon sugar
1 teaspoon vanilla extract
⅛ teaspoon cinnamon
½ teaspoon bottled lime juice
½ cup club soda

Mix well and add ice. This mixture will look very different from real cola, so the person making the taste test must be blindfolded. (If the person saw the mixture, he or she might not want to drink it!) Have your friend taste several different brands of cola, including your own, and try to identify your synthetic soda. Be sure all the sodas have ice in them.

You can carry this experiment further and develop your own formula that is much closer to real cola than the formula we've given you. Systematically vary the amounts of the ingredients and have your blindfolded friend check them against manufactured cola. For example, keep everything in the same proportion as we've given except vary the amount of sugar by half-teaspoonfuls until your soda is as sweet as the commercial soda. Then vary the amount of lime juice by half-teaspoonfuls, and so on.

6

The Chemical Senses

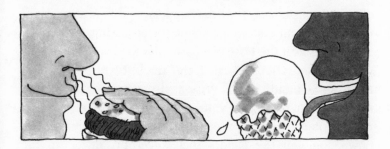

Food may look good enough to eat, but it will not be enjoyed properly unless it favorably impresses our chemical senses, namely taste and smell. Some scientists feel that our chemical senses are quite primitive and relatively unnecessary for our survival, compared to sight and hearing. We do in fact depend on sight and hearing for survival and communication. This is not as true for other species. Dogs, for example, have relatively poor vision and a keen sense of smell. Bees and other insects use "smell" to help locate flowers containing nectar, a substance essential to their survival. Nevertheless, taste and smell play an important role in the enjoyment of food, which is closely connected to good nutrition and to appetite. It is quite possible that, without our chemical senses, eating just to live would become a chore.

Since taste and smell are seemingly unimportant senses, we know less about them than the others. Scientists have not spent as much time studying them. Sight depends solely on light as a stimulus. Hearing and touch depend on changes in pressure. (Touch also responds to changes in temperature.) But no one has figured out just what makes sweet things taste sweet or bitter things taste bitter. Although we may know the molecular structure of a variety of sweet substances, they may appear so different we can't make a general statement about sweet-tasting molecules.

It seems as if the taste of a particular food is made up of a variety of sensations—basic taste, smell, texture, temperature, and "mouth feel." Vision also plays a part in the experience of tasting, as you will see from an experiment in this chapter. The basic idea behind this chapter is to break down some of the factors that, together, make up the experience of taste.

The branch of science that explores human experience is *psychology*. The study of a sense, of how we take in information about our environment, involves human subjects, and this creates complications. The study of taste, for example, is not as simple as presenting two kinds of food to a person and asking which is sweeter. The answer you get can be influenced by the order in which you present the foods, the tone of your voice when you ask the question, the subject's previous experience with the kind of food presented, and so on. The design of psychological experiments can become quite complicated as you try to control all these influences. For this reason, some of the experiments in this chapter use some simple statistics. You will make many presentations of food stimuli, in random order, and take an average of "correct" versus "incorrect" responses. We hope you will get some objective idea of the kind of taste your subject really experiences.

Smell Without Taste: Artificial Strawberry "Flavoring"

If flavors are nothing more than a mixture of chemicals, it should be possible to come very close to making a facsimile with the right combination of other ingredients. In this experiment you will test this proposition by putting together three substances that contain the basic aromatic chemicals of fresh strawberries.

Materials and Equipment

     measuring cup
     measuring spoons
     fresh green peas (shelled)
     brown sugar
     apple
     chopping bowl and knife, or a cutting board and knife,
          or a blender or food processor
     a blindfold
     a willing friend
     fresh strawberries

Procedure

We chopped up a mixture of about ½ cup fresh green peas with 2 tablespoons brown sugar and half a peeled and cored apple. (You can use a chopping bowl and knife, a cutting board and knife, or a blender or food processor to chop the ingredients.) Blindfold a friend and ask him or her to smell the mixture and identify the smell. Let him or her smell freshly chopped-up strawberries, and ask whether the two smells are the same.

Observations

When we blindfolded a friend and asked him to smell the mixture, he said it did indeed smell like strawberries. We are not certain of the exact proportions for an accurate synthetic reproduction, so we suggest that you try different proportions until you are pleased with the results. Use the suggested proportions as a starting point.

This mixture is completely edible. It does not, however, taste like strawberries. We found a two-year-old who didn't know any better and gobbled the whole experiment up.

What do your results tell you about the difference between taste and smell? How do you think food manufacturers might use this information to make processed foods seem more appealing?

TASTE WITHOUT SMELL: APPLE VERSUS POTATO VERSUS ONION

It's common knowledge that food tastes bland and uninteresting if you can't smell it. That's why it's a waste of time to prepare a gourmet meal for someone with a cold.

This experiment is designed to show just how important smell is to the sensation called "taste." Believe it or not, it's difficult to tell the difference between raw apple, potato, and onion when smell has been eliminated.

Materials and Equipment

  raw apple, peeled
  raw potato, peeled
  raw onion, peeled
  grater
  3 plates
  blindfold
  a willing friend
  nose clips (these can be purchased inexpensively at
      any drugstore)
  3 forks
  glass of water and basin
  pencil and paper
  paper bag

Procedure

Prepare the raw apple, potato, and onion by grating them onto plates. Use the finest part of the grater and be sure to rinse well for each kind of food. Grating reduces some of the difference in texture that can be a clue to the kind of food.

Blindfold a friend and put nose clips on him or her.

Present a sample by placing about ¼ teaspoon on the tongue with a fork. Tell your subject not to chew the sample, but to roll it around in the mouth, and then tell you what he or she thinks it is. The mouth should be rinsed out with water before the next presentation. The basin is for spitting out rinse water.

It is very important to present the samples in a random order—an order determined by chance. You can get a random order by assigning a number to each kind of food:

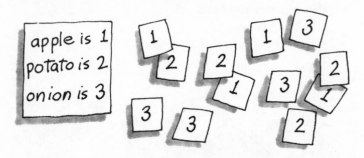

Suppose you are going to make 4 presentations of each sample. (You can, of course, make more.) Write each number on 4 tiny pieces of paper, giving a total of 12 pieces, then put them in a paper bag and shake. Draw out one piece of paper at a time and make a note of the order. This random or chance order is the order in which you present your samples.

Be sure your subject cannot tell from your reaction whether or not the response matches the stimulus presented. Remember, in nature there are no right or wrong answers!

Observations

Which sample was easiest to identify? Which two were confused the most? How important is the sense of smell?

Try this experiment on several people. Are some better than others at telling the differences?

Why is it important that you show no reaction to your subject's answers?

For Further Study

We have heard that without smell it is impossible to tell the difference between chocolate and vanilla ice cream. You can use the above procedure to find out. Also, you can use the procedure to see if temperature is a factor in the discrimination. Is it more difficult to distinguish between the flavors when the ice cream is frozen than when it is melted?

No Clues: Coke Versus 7-Up vs.

We have already investigated the mysterious flavor of Coca-Cola and learned that it is citrus-based. So is 7-Up. One obvious difference between them is color. Coke has caramel color added. If a person can't see the color of the soda, can Coke and 7-Up be confused? We designed this experiment to see for ourselves if there is indeed any other marked difference between the cola and the Uncola.

Materials and Equipment

> a large piece of heavy paper or cardboard (at least 2 square feet)
> 2 tall drinking glasses
> scissors
> Coca-Cola
> 7-Up
> ice
> drinking straws
> a scarf or towel
> a willing friend
> a blindfold
> pencil and paper
> nose clips (optional)

Procedure

We created a rather elaborate method in this experiment for preventing our subject from seeing the color of the beverage. We did this because experimental psychologists claim that no foolproof blindfold has ever been invented. It seems that peeking is always possible, especially when you're looking down your nose. However, if you want, you can use a regular blindfold instead.

Here's our method. Take a large piece of cardboard—large enough to extend out over the two glasses standing side by side. With scissors, poke two small, circular holes about 4 inches apart in the cardboard—make them just large enough to admit a straw. Rest the cardboard on top of the glasses, one containing Coke and the other containing 7-Up. Both sodas should contain ice, as temperature may be a factor. About 1 inch of straw should be sticking up

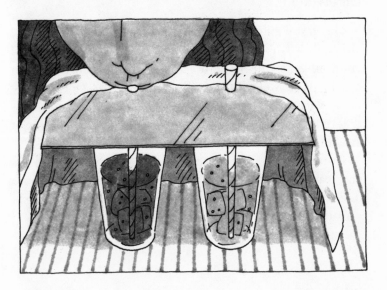

above the cardboard. Trim the straws to the right length with scissors. Drape a scarf or towel around the edge of the cardboard so that the glasses cannot be seen from the side.

Tell your subject that one straw goes to a Coke and the

other to a 7-Up. Instruct him or her to take a sip from each. The subject's lips should cover the extension of the straw completely and come in contact with the cardboard. This way the color of the beverage being sipped cannot be seen. The mouth should be rinsed out with water between sips.

Switch the glasses around several times for different trials. Don't tell your friend when the response is correct or incorrect. Record your results.

If your subject can tell the difference easily, try again using nose clips.

Observations

The taste difference between Coke and 7-Up is real, although it is much less than most people think. Some of your subjects will be better at telling the difference than others. How well did your first subject do? Does adding nose clips make the test more difficult? One major difference between the two soft drinks is that one is sweeter than the other. Can you tell which one?

Try the experiment on several people, using new straws and cardboard for each. Do older people have more difficulty telling Coke from 7-Up than young people? Taste sensitivity is often lessened with age.

SWEETENING MELONS

It's no news that strong tastes affect one another. Sourness, for example, is cut by sweetness. Make unsweetened lemonade, pour it into two glasses and add sugar to one. When you compare tastes you'll see that, although there is the same amount of sourness in both, the sweetened drink produces much less puckering.

Salt has an interesting effect on sweetness—tiny quantities of salt make sweet food taste sweeter. This phenomenon is called *flavor potentiation*, and you investigate it in
this experiment.

Materials and Equipment

> honeydew or cantaloupe melon (if melon is very
>   large, use 2 large pieces instead of halves)
> knife
> 2 plates
> salt
> pencil and paper
> a melon-loving friend
> lots of cereal boxes
> 2 forks
> glass of water

Procedure

Cut the melon in half. Keeping the halves separate, peel
them and cut them up into bite-size pieces. You will have
two equal batches of fruit.

Spread out the pieces of each group on a plate. Sprinkle
one group lightly with salt. The salted melon is group one;
the unsalted group two. Prepare a sheet to collect data with
the headings *Group 1* and *Group 2*.

You should set up a barricade of cereal boxes or keep the
two plates of melon pieces on your lap under the table so
your subject can't see which group you take a piece from.

Tell your subject that some of the pieces are sweeter
than others. He or she is to eat the piece, tell you if it is

"sweeter" or "less sweet," and take a sip of water between pieces to rinse out the mouth. Use forks to feed melon pieces to the subject.

You must present pieces in a random sequence. Here is one you can use: 1,2,2,1,1,1,1,2,2,1,2,2,1,2,1,2. If you have more pieces than this sequence, start the sequence at the beginning again.

Record your subject's responses in the appropriate columns on your data sheet.

Observations

Did your subject have difficulty noticing a difference between salted and unsalted melon? Did your subject mention that any of the melon tasted salty? Our subject had no problem detecting the difference—salty melon was identified as "sweeter."

Many people salt grapefuit. As this experiment shows, there is method in their madness.

THE ARTICHOKE PHENOMENON

Artichokes are not your usual standard vegetable for family meals. For one thing, they are quite a bother to eat. You peel the leaves off with your fingers, dip the tender lower ends in some kind of sauce, and scrape them against your lower teeth. Not exactly good table manners. Knowing how to eat artichokes is evidence of worldly knowledge. And artichokes have come to be considered a treat for gourmets.

Recently a famous chef announced that fine wines should not be served with artichokes. This may not seem like an earth-shaking pronouncement until you understand that the kind of gourmets who enjoy eating artichokes in fine restaurants drink a different kind of fine wine with each course. The famous chef would not put a ban on wine with

artichokes without good reason. And the reason is that artichokes have a very peculiar effect on the tongue. In this experiment you will study this strange artichoke effect.

Materials and Equipment

1 fresh globe artichoke
knife
small saucepan and cover (not aluminum)
plate and fork
a willing friend
glass of water
watch with a second hand

Procedure

First prepare the artichoke. Wash it by running water on it while holding it right side up. Turn it upside down to drain. Slice off the stem so it has a flat bottom.

Put about 2 inches of water in the bottom of a saucepan. Place the artichoke in it right side up. Cover and let the water boil until the "heart" or base of the artichoke is tender. Check for tenderness by sticking a fork into the vegetable. Depending on the size of the artichoke, it will take anywhere from 20 to 40 minutes to reach a tender state. If the water seems to be boiling off, add more. Allow the artichoke to cool to room temperature before performing the experiment.

You can use the leaves for this experiment, but we found the effect easier to measure with the heart. Cut the leaves off the heart and scrape out the bristly "choke." Artichokes are related to thistles and the choke is usually not eaten. Cut the heart into quarters.

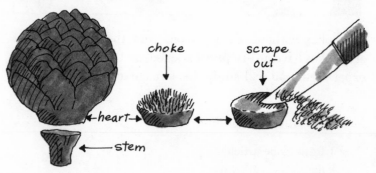

Have your subject sip from a glass of water. Then have him or her chew a quarter of an artichoke heart and hold it in the mouth for 2 minutes without swallowing it. Then have the subject sip the water and tell you how it tastes.

Scientific studies show that most, but not all, people find that water now tastes sweet. If your subject does find that the water tastes sweet, have him or her continue to sip water so you can time the length of the effect. Have the subject tell you when water tastes tasteless again.

This experiment should be repeated several times for more accurate results. Try it on several subjects, using more artichokes as needed. When the experiment is finished, you can eat the leaves, as described above, dipping them in mayonnaise or melted butter if you wish.

Observations

How long did the effect last? Try having your subject sip milk instead of water. Does the subject report that milk tastes sweet?

Chemicals in artichokes affect the taste buds in some mysterious way so that anything eaten or drunk while eating an artichoke, or shortly afterward, tastes sweet. Artichokes apparently can prevent a person from tasting the true flavor of a fine wine, which explains why the famous chef refused to serve wine with this vegetable.

Manufacturers of dietetic foods are always on the lookout for new low-calorie sweeteners. Do your results show why they have been interested in isolating the chemical that causes the mysterious artichoke effect?

For Further Study

See if freezing, canning, or marinating affects the phenomenon by repeating the experiment with frozen, canned, and marinated artichoke hearts. We have read that there are other chemicals that alter the tongue to produce different aftertastes. Table salt makes water taste bitter-sour, sugar makes water taste bitter, and lemon juice and quinine water make water taste sweet. Experiment to find out if this is indeed true.

MAPPING THE TONGUE

The several hundred tiny bumps on your tongue, called *papillae*, are organs that have the special job of sensing the basic tastes of sweet, sour, salt, or bitter. Each contains more than 200 tiny sensing cells called "taste buds." When a sweet chemical comes in contact with a taste bud sensitive to sweet chemicals, the nerve cells respond to the sweet stimulus and send the message "sweet" to your brain. Taste buds are specific in their response. That is, a taste bud responsive to bitter flavors will not respond to sweet.

Taste buds are scattered over the surface of the tongue. But there are also a few under the tongue and on the inside of the cheeks. For many years it has been believed that some areas of the tongue are more sensitive to certain taste sensations than others. Recently this belief has been challenged, and scientists have not yet come to any definite conclusions. The idea of this experiment is to see if, indeed, certain areas of the tongue are more responsive to one particular taste than to another.

In this experiment you present four taste stimuli to four areas of the tongue. As a control, you also present water. This means that there will be five stimulus presentations in a random order to four tongue locations in a random order. Randomization makes the procedure for this experiment the most complicated in the book. Read through the entire experiment and make sure you fully understand it before you do it.

Materials and Equipment

>   sugar
>   salt
>   cream of tartar
>   measuring spoons
>   spoons for stirring
>   5 glasses
>   black coffee
>   paper, tape, scissors, pen
>   5 identical small brand-new paint brushes
>   a willing friend
>   nose clips
>   a sheet
>   various cereal boxes or props to drape the sheet
>   over
>   glass of water
>   basin for spitting out mouth rinse
>   pencil and data sheets

Procedure

First, the setup: There is no attempt in this experiment to make the four basic tastes equal in strength. Mix about 2 teaspoons of sugar in half a glass of water. Do the same with salt and with cream of tartar (sour). The bitter flavoring is black coffee, which should be at room temperature. (Quinine water can also be used to represent bitter, but it contains some sugar.) Label each glass as follows:

sweet is labeled #5
salt is labeled #6
sour is labeled #7
bitter is labeled #8
water is labeled #9

Put a new paint brush into each glass.

Now get your subject ready. Put on nose clips to eliminate the sense of smell. This is extremely important if you are using coffee as the bitter flavor; coffee gives off aromas that will tip off your subject. Tie the sheet around your subject's neck. Drape the sheet over cereal boxes to form a horizontal bib under which you put the five glasses containing the different taste solutions. Your subject must not be able to identify the taste by seeing the general location of the brush you use.

Next, make sure your subject can properly identify the five stimuli. Ask your subject to taste the contents of each glass and identify the taste. Have him or her rinse out the mouth with water and spit the rinse into a basin between tastes.

Tell your subject that you will be presenting the solutions on different points on the tongue by touching it with a brush wetted with one of the five solutions. As soon as the subject feels the brush he or she is to make one of six responses: "sweet," "salty," "sour," "bitter," "water," or "I don't know." Again, it is extremely important that you give away no clues as to the correctness of the response.

Collecting the Data

Have a prepared data sheet and pencil in front of you. Here's how the data sheet works. The tongue is divided into four areas labeled 1, 2, 3, 4, as shown in the picture.

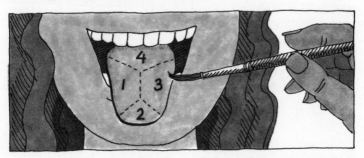

Each area will receive each of the 5 stimulus tastes 4 times, making a total of 80 presentations or trials. We have prepared a coded table that ensures that the order of presentation of the taste solution is random and the order of the part of the tongue stimulated is also random.

TABLE OF RANDOM STIMULUS AND AREA PRESENTATIONS

TONGUE LOCATION	TASTE SOLUTION	RESPONSE	TONGUE LOCATION	TASTE SOLUTION	RESPONSE
4	5		3	7	
4	6		2	5	
2	5		3	6	
2	7		3	8	
2	6		3	9	
1	8		3	6	
2	5		1	7	
3	7		1	7	
4	8		2	8	
4	6		1	7	
4	5		1	6	
3	5		3	8	
2	6		1	5	
2	9		2	6	
2	7		4	9	
3	5		3	5	
3	9		1	6	
3	9		3	7	
4	6		4	5	
4	9		2	8	
1	6		1	8	
4	6		3	8	
2	8		2	9	
2	9		2	5	
4	8		2	6	
3	8		3	6	
3	7		2	7	
1	9		4	7	
2	7		3	5	
4	8		1	5	
4	7		3	9	
4	5		2	8	
4	8		1	5	
1	6		4	9	
4	7		4	9	
1	8		1	7	
3	6		1	9	
4	7		1	5	
2	9		1	8	
1	9		1	9	

Here's how to read the table: Numerals 1, 2, 3, and 4 stand for areas of the tongue. Numerals 5, 6, 7, 8, and 9 stand for sweet, salty, sour, bitter, and water. The first trial on the table reads 4——5. This means that you dab the back part of the tongue, area 4, with solution #5, or sugar water. The numerals 2——7 mean the tip of the tongue is stimulated with a dab of sour water. Numerals 1——8 mean the right side of the tongue is dabbed with black coffee.

Copy the table in columns on ruled paper. In the blank column titled "Response," use numerals to record what your subject says. The numerals for responses are:

> 5 — "sweet"
> 6 — "salty"
> 7 — "sour"
> 8 — "bitter"
> 9 — "water"
> 0 — "I don't know"

When we did the experiment, our first trial read 450. This means that the back of the tongue was dabbed with sugar water and the subject responded "I don't know." A reading of 277 means that the tip of the tongue was dabbed with sour solution and the subject said "sour."

At this point, if all is perfectly clear, go and gather your data.

Analyzing the Data

At the end of the procedure you will have 80 numbers that need interpretation. These numbers are called *raw data*. Somewhere in the raw data is an indication of order. You now have to do what many scientists spend a great deal of time doing—rearranging the raw data to see if they have some meaning. This act is called analyzing the data, and in the world of professional scientists computers are programmed to do much of the processing. You will perform two operations on your data. The first is designed to show if one part of the tongue is more sensitive *on the average* to one particular taste than to others.

To do this, take a fresh sheet of paper and make four columns, one for each area of the tongue:

Look through your raw data for match-ups between stimulus and response. If you should find, for example, 255, write the word *sweet* under column 2. This means that the sweet stimulus was correctly identified on area 2 of the tongue. Ignore all the water stimuli. You are looking for responses for particular taste sensations.

After you have finished entering all the names of the correct stimulus-response pairs, count up the number for each taste for each area of the tongue. Remember that each taste was presented to each area four times, so the most correct responses any tongue area can have is four. In our experiment sweet and sour were correctly identified by the tip of the tongue every time they were presented. Bitter was identified correctly three out of four times. We concluded that the tip was more sensitive to sweet and sour than it was to bitter.

Incorrect Responses			
1	2	3	4
bitter— water	sour— salty	salty— bitter	bitter— I don't know
salty— sour			

The second operation on your data is to show if one area of the tongue is more sensitive *in general* than other areas, and if any tastes are especially often confused. Again make four columns, one for each area of the tongue. Look through your raw data for *incorrect* responses. Write down in each tongue-area column the stimulus and the incorrect response. For example, 189 means you write "bitter-water" under the column indicating the right side of the tongue. The number 480 means you write "bitter–I don't know" under the column for the back of the tongue.

Observations

If you wish, you can average the findings for columns 1 and 3, since the tongue is symmetrical. Keep in mind that in this situation the total number of presentations for any taste solution is eight rather than four. Which section or sections most accurately identified sweet? Sour? Salty? Bitter? Which taste was most difficult to identify? Which part of the tongue seemed to be most sensitive? Which section of the tongue made the fewest correct determinations? (Look at your second table for answers to these two questions.)

Scientific studies have shown that sweet and salt are best sensed at the tip of the tongue, bitter is best tasted at the back of the tongue, sour is best tasted along the sides, and sour and salt are often confused. How do your findings compare with those of professional scientists?

About the Author

VICKI COBB attended the University of Wisconsin on a Ford Foundation Early Admissions Scholarship, then continued her education at Barnard College, where she received her B.A. degree, and at Columbia University Teachers College, where she was awarded an M.A. degree.

After an early career as a science teacher, Ms. Cobb turned to writing. In addition to film strips and other educational aids, she has written scripts for network television, and was the creator and principal personality of "The Science Game," an educational television series. Ms. Cobb is the author of a number of books for young people, most of which are on scientific subjects.

About the Illustrator

GIULIO MAESTRO studied at Pratt Graphics Center and at Cooper Union, where he received a Bachelor of Fine Arts degree. After five years as an assistant art director/designer in advertising, he became a full-time free-lance illustrator of children's books. His work has been cited for merit and exhibited by the New York Society of Illustrators and the American Institute of Graphic Arts.

ALSO BY VICKI COBB

Science Experiments You Can Eat

Arts and Crafts You Can Eat

Magic . . . Naturally!